THE AMERICAN KENNEL CLUB'S
Meet the
Shih Tzu ™

W9-ATZ-126

The Responsible Dog Owner's Handbook

AKC's
Meet the Breeds Series
I-5 Publishing, LLC™

AN OFFICIAL PUBLICATION OF — AKC — THE AMERICAN KENNEL CLUB

AMERICAN KENNEL CLUB

Brought to you by The American Kennel Club and The American Shih Tzu Club.

Lead Editor: Lindsay Hanks
Art Director: Cindy Kassebaum
Production Manager: Laurie Panaggio
Production Supervisor: Jessica Jaensch
Production Coordinator: Leah Rosalez

I-5 PUBLISHING, LLC™
Chief Executive Officer: Mark Harris
Chief Financial Officer: Nicole Fabian
Vice President, Chief Content Officer: June Kikuchi
General Manager, I-5 Press: Christopher Reggio
Editorial Director, I-5 Press: Andrew DePrisco
Art Director, I-5 Press: Mary Ann Kahn
Digital General Manager: Melissa Kauffman
Production Director: Laurie Panaggio
Production Manager: Jessica Jaensch
Marketing Director: Lisa MacDonald

Photographs by: Blackhawk Productions (Dwight Dyke): 9, 26, 40, 115; Gina Cioli/BowTie Studio: Cover, 8, 10, 28, 33, 39, 42, 75, 79, 96, 124; Close Encounters of the Furry Kind: Cover, Back Cover, 1, 3-4, 6-7, 11, 12, 14-15, 16, 17, 18-19, 20, 21, 22, 23, 24-25, 29, 31, 32, 34, 35, 36-37, 38, 46, 47, 53, 54, 55, 56, 57, 58-59, 60, 61, 64, 66, 67, 68-69, 71, 72, 73, 77, 78, 82, 84, 85, 87, 88-89, 90, 91, 92, 97, 98-99, 112, 118, 120, 127; Fox Hill Photo: 27, 41, 44, 48-49, 51, 52, 62, 63, 65, 70, 80-81, 86, 93, 94, 95, 100, 101, 103, 104, 108; Infocus by Miguel (Miguel Betancourt): 119, 121; Jerry Shulman: 30, 43, 74, 107, 110-111, 117

Library of Congress Cataloging-in-Publication Data

The American Kennel Club's meet the Shih tzu : the responsible dog owner's handbook.
    p. cm. -- (Akc's meet the breeds series)
  Includes bibliographical references and index.
  ISBN 978-1-935484-73-8
  1. Shih tzu. I. American Kennel Club.
  SF429.S64A44 2011
  636.76--dc23
                            2011023963

This book has been published with the intent to provide accurate and authoritative information in regard to the subject matter within. While every precaution has been taken in the preparation of this book, the author and publisher expressly disclaim any responsibility for any errors, omissions, or adverse effects arising from the use or application of the information contained herein. The techniques and suggestions are used at the reader's discretion and are not to be considered a substitute for veterinary care. If you suspect a medical problem, consult your veterinarian.

I-5 Publishing, LLC™
3 Burroughs, Irvine, CA 92618
www.facebook.com/i5press
www.i5publishing.com

Printed and bound in the United States

17 16 15 14   5 6 7 8 9 10

Meet Your New Dog

Welcome to *Meet the Shih Tzu*. Whether you're a long-time Shih Tzu owner, or you've just gotten your first puppy, we wish you a lifetime of happiness and enjoyment with your new pet.

In this book, you'll learn about the history of the breed, receive tips on feeding, grooming and training, and learn about all the fun you can have with your dog. The American Kennel Club and I-5 Press hope that this book serves as a useful guide on the lifelong journey you'll take with your canine companion.

The Shih Tzu is one of the most popular breeds in the United States—in no small part due to the breed's lively, friendly nature and beautiful, luxurious coat. Owned and cherished by millions across America, Shih Tzu dogs thrive as house pets and companions, yet they also enjoy taking part in therapy dog work and a variety of dog sports, including Conformation (dog shows), Obedience, Rally®, and Agility.

Thousands of Shih Tzu have also earned the AKC Canine Good Citizen® certification by demonstrating their good manners at home and in the community. We hope that you and your Shih Tzu will become involved in AKC events, too! Learn how to get involved at www.akc.org/events, or find a training club in your area at www.akc.org/events/trainingclubs.cfm.

We encourage you to connect with other Shih Tzu owners on the AKC website (www.akc.org), Facebook (www.facebook.com/americankennelclub) and Twitter (@akcdoglovers). Also visit the American Shih Tzu Club, Inc. (www.americanshihtzuclub.org or search Facebook for American Shih Tzu Club, Inc.), the national parent club for the Shih Tzu, to learn about the breed from reputable exhibitors and breeders.

Enjoy *Meet the Shih Tzu*!

Sincerely,

Dennis B. Sprung
AKC President and CEO

Contents

CHAPTER ONE

Great Pets in Small Packages

Are you looking for a thoroughly charming, highly attractive breed to join you in the daily hubbub of modern family life? Then look no further than the enchanting Shih Tzu. If your own personality attracts people of a friendly disposition, you are sure to love the Shih Tzu, whose affectionate character makes him an ideal companion.

If you want a beautiful dog to take into the show ring, you really need not look any further

Popularity Contest

The Shih Tzu has been one of the ten most popular dogs in the United States for more than a decade, according to the American Kennel Club. That's one popular dog! To register your Shih Tzu with the AKC, fill out the Dog Registration Application you received when you bought your puppy, and simply mail it to the AKC in North Carolina, or register online through www.akc.org.

A LIKELY MATCH

The old cliché holds true: people find pets that best suit their personalities. The ideal Shih Tzu person is likely to have the same outgoing and affectionate personality traits found in the Shih Tzu. Combine that with the breed's intelligence, and you have a dog that is happy to work on his own initiative.

This can make for fascinating entertainment for the owner—often seeing your Shih Tzu figure things out in his head, planning his strategy for getting what he wants. Unlike many easily bored dogs that constantly need to be given things to do, a Shih Tzu will make his own amusement.

It should go without saying that the Shih Tzu must live in the home with you; this is definitely not an outdoor breed. He can be perfectly content with just one person, to whom he will undoubtedly bestow affection and loyalty, provided this is reciprocated with kindness. Equally, if you have a fairly active household, your Shih Tzu will probably be happy to join in with most activities. However, you must allow your Shih Tzu to decide how much he wants to be involved. If he prefers to be left out of whatever is going on, that should be his prerogative. Give your dog time and space to spend by himself, and he will more thoroughly enjoy the time you spend together.

The Shih Tzu is independent, meaning he craves his time alone just as much as he wishes to bond with you. Shih Tzu usually enjoy the company of people of all ages, including children, but you should always bear in mind that children must be taught to respect dogs. Smaller dogs like the Shih Tzu can be easily stepped on or injured by children who play too roughly or fail to watch out while running around the house. Shih Tzu love affection and can be very tolerant, but children who don't know better may pull at the breed's long, luxuriant coat and cause pain. If you bring a Shih Tzu into a home with children, be sure to put your parenting skills to good use and teach your kids gentleness and care. Even a tolerant Shih Tzu can only be expected to withstand so much handling. No dog's patience should ever be tested to the limits.

The bottom line is: you must never, under any circumstances, treat your Shih Tzu harshly. Don't even use harsh words when you get frustrated or upset at his misbehavior. If you are capable of giving this smart little dog the respect he deserves, you will have a wonderful companion for years to come.

EASY KEEPING

Small in stature, the Shih Tzu doesn't need a marathon walk each day. But they are an active breed that loves to take a good walk when given the opportunity. So, if you have no yard where your Shih Tzu can roam around, be sure to take him on a couple of walks throughout the day, to make sure he gets plenty of exercise.

Independent, affectionate, and loyal—the Shih Tzu makes for a great companion animal.

Oftentimes, people assume that all small dogs are noisy, barking all day long. Alert in every way, the Shih Tzu pays attention to what is happening around him and will certainly pick up on nearby sounds. However, this is not a particularly noisy breed, so you shouldn't anticipate encountering trouble with neighbors complaining about a "barky" dog, as is sometimes the case with some other small breeds.

PREPARE TO GROOM

Although the Shih Tzu is a rather independent breed, one area requires your attention: coat care. With such a unique long coat, the Shih Tzu's hair can easily become a tangled mess without your intervention to keep it presentable.

Be prepared to pay close attention to your Shih Tzu's long hair, even if you choose to keep it short. It's simply par for the course in owning this breed. The Shih Tzu's coat sheds little, unlike that of many other long-haired breeds. Fortunately, this means that you won't find large quantities of dog hair around your home. However, the dog's coat will form knots if left unattended, so you need to be prepared to spend time daily to groom your pet Shih Tzu. It's a major part of this breed's daily care needs.

There is no doubt that keeping the Shih Tzu's coat glorious requires plenty of time and attention, but grooming can be calming and therapeutic for both parties. The breed should be especially appealing to the hairstylists among us!

Did You Know?

The word *Shih Tzu* means "lion," and the breed lives up to its name. Although this dog is sweet and playful, he is not afraid to stand up for himself. In Chinese, the breed's full name is Tibetan Shih Tzu Kou, or Tibetan Lion Dog.

Be Responsible

Getting a dog is exciting, but it's also a huge responsibility. That's why it's important to educate yourself on all that is involved in being a good pet owner. As a part of the Canine Good Citizen® test, the AKC has a "Responsible Dog Owner's Pledge," which states:

I will be responsible for my dog's health needs.

☐ I will provide routine veterinary care, including check-ups and vaccines.

☐ I will offer adequate nutrition through proper diet and clean water at all times.

☐ I will give daily exercise and regularly bathe and groom.

I will be responsible for my dog's safety.

☐ I will properly control my dog by providing fencing where appropriate, by not letting my dog run loose, and by using a leash in public.

☐ I will ensure that my dog has some form of identification when appropriate (which may include collar tags, tattoos, or microchip identification).

☐ I will provide adequate supervision when my dog and children are together.

I will not allow my dog to infringe on the rights of others.

☐ I will not allow my dog to run loose in the neighborhood.

☐ I will not allow my dog to be a nuisance to others by barking while in the yard, in a hotel room, etc.

☐ I will pick up and properly dispose of my dog's waste in all public areas, such as on the grounds of hotels, on sidewalks, in parks, etc.

☐ I will pick up and properly dispose of my dog's waste in wilderness areas, on hiking trails, on campgrounds, and in off-leash parks.

I will be responsible for my dog's quality of life.

☐ I understand that basic training is beneficial to all dogs.

☐ I will give my dog attention and playtime.

☐ I understand that owning a dog is a commitment in time and caring.

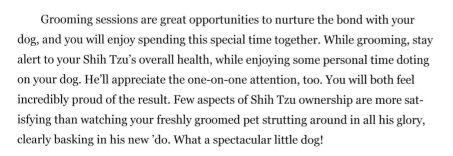

Grooming sessions are great opportunities to nurture the bond with your dog, and you will enjoy spending this special time together. While grooming, stay alert to your Shih Tzu's overall health, while enjoying some personal time doting on your dog. He'll appreciate the one-on-one attention, too. You will both feel incredibly proud of the result. Few aspects of Shih Tzu ownership are more satisfying than watching your freshly groomed pet strutting around in all his glory, clearly basking in his new 'do. What a spectacular little dog!

Coat care is a very important aspect of Shih Tzu ownership. Sure, it's time consuming, but consider it bonding time with your dog. The result will be absolutely beautiful.

OUTSIDE THE HOME

The Shih Tzu is a wonderful companion, and his dazzling appearance, with that magnificent coat and elegant topknot, makes him highly popular as a show dog.

Some Shih Tzu take part in agility and obedience work, and their charming personalities make them good candidates for therapy work, too. However, the Shih Tzu is just as delighted to live a leisurely life around the home and will show his love for you in so many ways that you will know you've made the right decision by letting him enter your life.

THINK ABOUT IT

Getting a dog is a really big decision. It is a long-term commitment, which you should discuss with every member of your family or household before making a final decision. Make sure the decision is based on what's best for you, your family, and the dog—not done on impulse to bring a cute new dog into your home.

Don't rush into dog ownership! Having a dog will greatly affect your life and everyday activities. Once you decide to bring a Shih Tzu into your home, learn all you can and prepare for the years to come of companionship with your new best friend.

Meet the Shih Tzu and More!

A great place to see Shih Tzu and more than 200 other dog and cat breeds is at AKC Meet the Breeds®, hosted by the American Kennel Club and presented by Pet Partners, Inc. Not only can you see dogs, cats, puppies, and kittens of all sizes, you can also talk to experts in each of the breeds. Meet the Breeds features demonstration rings to watch events with law-enforcement K9s, grooming, agility, and obedience. You also can browse the more than 100 vendor booths for every imaginable product for you and your pet.

It's great fun for the whole family. Meet the Breeds takes place in the fall in New York City. For more information, check out www.meetthebreeds.com.

At a Glance ...

The ideal Shih Tzu owner wants a charming, small dog that is affectionate, bright, and friendly.

. . . .

A Shih Tzu person has time to care for his dog's elegant coat or else is willing to take the dog to a professional groomer. Whatever the situation, the Shih Tzu owner understands that his dog's coat care cannot be neglected.

. . . .

A Shih Tzu owner is responsible for the safety and careful handling of his small dog and for teaching others how to appropriately interact with the dog, as well.

. . . .

A Shih Tzu person loves to have his dog in the home as a true part of the family and family life.

CHAPTER TWO

Far East Fancy

The Shih Tzu is among the most ancient of dog breeds. There are hundreds of canine breeds in the world today, and still others that have become extinct over time. Oftentimes, ancient breeds were bred together to create new breeds, including some of the most popular dogs around today like the Shih Tzu. According to the American Kennel Club's registration statistics, the Shih Tzu is currently one of the most popular breeds in the United States.

Small in stature, the Shih Tzu typically stands only 9 to 10½ inches fully grown.

What makes the Shih Tzu unique among his peers? Fans of the breed praise his regal stature and striking good looks. Tracing his lineage to China and Tibet with what's believed to be Pekingese and Lhasa Apso or Tibetan mountain dog ancestry, the Shih Tzu has developed a look and personality all his own. These characteristics unify all Shih Tzu in what is called a breed standard, which is a written description of what each dog should look like and what his temperament should be.

BRED TO PERFECTION

So, who determines what should be included in the breed standard? Within the American Kennel Club, every dog breed has a national club called a parent club, whose responsibility is to protect and promote its breed. One of the most

Coat of Many Colors

What color Shih Tzu should you get? Take your pick! The American Kennel Club accepts all colors, including solid red, black, and any combination of gold, red, or silver with white. According to the breed standard, all colors are permissible and to be considered equal in the show ring.

AMERICAN KENNEL CLUB™

important aspects of that job is to decide on the breed standard, describing the ideal specimen of the breed. That's why all Shih Tzu look and act like Shih Tzu, and all Bulldogs and Chihuahuas look and act like their own breeds. The Shih Tzu's parent club is the American Shih Tzu Club (www.americanshihtzuclub.org) and is a member of the American Kennel Club.

Every time a Shih Tzu competes in a dog show, the judge uses the breed standard to decide how closely each dog matches the description. The judge then selects as the winner the dog that most closely conforms to the standard on that day.

The dogs that earn championships at shows are the dogs that breeders choose to continue their line. In fact, the purpose of a dog show is to compare breeding stock and determine which animals are most suitable for breeding. Breeders use the breed standard as the blueprint to create the next generation of Shih Tzu, always trying to improve their line and get closer to the standard of perfection.

As pups, Shih Tzu are even smaller, making careful handling of utmost importance when you first bring one home.

TOY GROUP

The Shih Tzu is classified by the AKC as a member of the Toy Group. All Toy breeds are small in size and kept as companion pets. Living up to their names, Toy dogs are a joy to play with and have around the home. The AKC describes the main function of the group as "to embody sheer delight." And that's just what the Shih Tzu does. The breed's diminutive size and charming expression most certainly fit the bill. Not all small dog breeds belong to the Toy group, but every Toy dog is petite.

The Shih Tzu is believed to descend from many Eastern breeds, including the Pekingese and the Lhaso Apso.

Don't let their tiny stature fool you, though; most Toy breeds are hardy little fellows. Call it what you want—a Napoleon complex or overcompensation for their size—but Toy breeds often have an inherent, instinctive response to protect themselves.

Alert, lively, and a bit stubborn, the Shih Tzu is one assertive little dog. The word *Shih Tzu* means "lion," and these dogs certainly aren't afraid to stand up for themselves when they feel threatened. Courageous as they are, Shih Tzu have sweet and playful natures and are perfectly peaceful when they feel at ease. For that reason, it is important to evaluate your home environment before bringing one home. The Shih Tzu may not be the best choice for a busy household full of noise or active children.

Anatomy of a Shih Tzu

WITHERS

BACK

STOP

MUZZLE

CHEST

ELBOW

BRISKET

CROUP

HIP

LOIN

HOCK

The Shih Tzu in Brief

COUNTRY OF ORIGIN:
Tibet and China

ORIGINAL USE:
Royal companion and palace pet

GROUP:
Toy

AVERAGE LIFE SPAN:
13 to 15 years

COAT:
Double-coated with a long, silky, flowing outer coat and a soft, dense undercoat.

COLOR:
Any coat color is acceptable, including solid red, black, and combinations of gold, red, or silver with white.

GROOMING:
Long-coated dogs require extensive grooming, including daily brushing and frequent bathing. Clipped coats need twice-weekly brushing and bathing about every three weeks. Keep the eyes, nose, and ears clean; clip nails and brush teeth weekly.

HEIGHT/WEIGHT:
Ideally, 9 to 10 ½ inches; about 9 to 16 pounds

TRAINABILITY:
Moderate

PERSONALITY:
Sweet, trusting, curious, happy, sociable, and easy-going.

ACTIVITY LEVEL:
Moderate

GOOD WITH OTHER PETS:
Yes, excellent with both dogs and cats. Generally not aggressive toward small pets, but use caution.

NATIONAL BREED CLUB:
American Shih Tzu Club; akotze@charter .net; www.americanshihtzuclub.org

RESCUE:
American Shih Tzu Club; toydogrsq@aol .com; www.americanshihtzuclub.org

Toy dogs will always be popular with city dwellers and people without much living space. They make ideal pets for people who live in condos or apartments, as well as perfect lap warmers on chilly nights. Other benefits of small-breed dogs include less shedding, typically smaller messes around the house, and a smaller quantity of food. And training aside, it's still easier to control a 10-pound dog than it is to control one ten times that size.

FACE IT

One of the breed's most striking characteristics is its petite muzzle, with wide nostrils and a steep stop (where the nose and foreface meet). This facial shape defines the Shih Tzu as a brachycephalic breed, meaning literally that the dog is short nosed and has a short muzzle. But unlike other brachycephalic dog breeds, such as the Pug and the Pekingese, the Shih Tzu's muzzle should not be wrinkled. No two dogs are the same, and one Shih Tzu's face and body may differ slightly from another. But for the most part, all should resemble each other. However, you may see dogs whose noses look level, while others' are slightly tipped; but none of their noses should be pointed downward. Feel free to look a gift dog in the mouth. Shih Tzu have

One of the Shih Tzu's most defining characteristics is his facial features. The word *chrysanthemum* is used a lot to describe the outward growth of hair around the face from the nose out.

wide mouths, and their teeth may be level but are usually slightly undershot.

Shih Tzu have large, dark, round eyes that are placed well apart but not prominent on the face. Their hair falls well over their eyes, but it is typically pulled into a topknot when not in a pet trim. The upward growth of hair on the nose creates a look similar to the rounded bloom of a flower, often described as a "chrysanthemum-like" effect.

A PIECE OF HISTORY

A member of the Toy Group breed classification, the Shih Tzu was first recognized by the American Kennel Club in 1969.

SMALL BUT MIGHTY

Standing between 9 and 10½ inches tall, Shih Tzu have delighted their owners—often members of their societies' wealthy ruling class—for centuries. Most Shih Tzu weigh in around 9 to 16 pounds.

But just try telling the Shih Tzu he's tiny. He may be small, but the Shih Tzu is quite sturdy compared to many other breeds that are about the same size. A surprisingly heavy dog for its size, the breed standard calls for a "sturdy, abundantly coated dog with distinctly arrogant carriage." The Shih Tzu proudly carries his broad head high, with round wide eyes looking straight ahead. It's like he knows his ancestors held their place in Chinese court centuries before.

The Shih Tzu has seen broad changes in height over the centuries. In the past, extremely small dogs were particularly favored by some, but now the breed has evened out in size, and the tiny specimens are few and far between. A proper Shih Tzu will conform to the breed standard. The AKC allows for a mature Shih Tzu to range from 9 to 16 pounds, while standards in the United Kingdom and continental Europe allow a range of 10 to 18 pounds, with 10 to 16 pounds specified as ideal.

ON THE SURFACE

The Shih Tzu's long, flowing double coat is the breed's most distinctive feature. Fanciers consider the abundant coat as the breed's crowning glory. There may be a lot of it, but the Shih Tzu's hair won't get all over your house. It is long and dense, with a good undercoat. Although a slight wave is permitted, the coat should not be curly. The topknot, heavily coated ears, and a well-plumed

Give your Shih Tzu plenty of outdoor playtime, like any other dog, but remember to groom his coat afterward to avoid matting.

Shih Tzu Breed Standard

AMERICAN
KENNEL CLUB™

OVERALL: The Shih Tzu is a sturdy, lively, alert Toy dog with a long flowing double coat. He has a distinctively arrogant carriage with head well up and tail curved over the back. Although there has always been considerable size variation, the Shih Tzu must be compact and solid, carrying good weight and substance.

PROPORTION

The length between the withers and root of tail is slightly longer than height at withers. The Shih Tzu must never appear leggy, nor dumpy or squatty.

HEAD

The head shound be round, broad, and wide between the eyes. The expression should be warm, sweet, wide-eyed, friendly and trusting. An overall well-balanced and pleasant expression supercedes the importance of individual parts. Large, round eyes should not be prominent, but placed well apart, looking straight ahead. They should be very dark; lighter on liver pigmented dogs and blue pigmented dogs. Large ears are set slightly below the crown of the skull; heavily coated. Must have a domed skull and definite stop. Square, short, unwrinkled muzzle with good cushioning, set no lower than bottom eye rim; never downturned. Nostrils are broad, wide, and open. Nose, lips, eye rims are black on all colors, except liver on liver-pigmented dogs and blue on blue-pigmented dogs. The bite is undershot. Jaw is broad and wide. A missing tooth or slightly misaligned teeth should not be too severely penalized.

NECK

Of utmost importance is an overall well-balanced dog with no exaggerated features. The neck is well set-on, flowing smoothly into the shoulders; of sufficient length to permit a natural high head carriage and in balance with the height and length of the dog.

TOPLINE

The topline should be level. The body short-coupled and sturdy with no waist or tuck-up. The Shih Tzu is slightly longer than tall. The chest is broad and deep, however, not barrel-chested. Depth of rib cage should extend to just below the elbow. Distance from elbow to withers is a little greater than from elbow to ground.

TAIL

The tail is set on high, heavily plumed, and carried in a curve well over the back. Too loose, too tight, too flat, or too low set a tail is undesirable.

FOREQUARTERS

The shoulders should be well-angulated, well laid-back, well laid-in, fitting smoothly into the body. Straight, well-boned, muscular legs are set well-apart and under the chest, with elbows set close to the body. Feet are firm, well-padded, and point straight ahead.

HINDQUARTERS

Angulation of hindquarters should be in balance with forequarters. Legs must be well-boned, muscular, and straight when viewed from rear with well-bent stifles, not close set but in line with forequarters.

COAT

Coat should be luxurious, double-coated, dense, long, and flowing. Slight wave is permissible. Hair on top of head is tied up. Feet, bottom of coat, and anus may be trimmed for neatness and to facilitate movement. All colors and markings are permissible and to be considered equally.

—Excerpts from the Shih Tzu Breed Standard

tail help to complete a highly attractive picture. All colors are permissible, but in parti-colors; a white blaze on the forehead and white tip to the tail are highly desirable—markings that were beloved by the Tibetans.

In overall balance, the Shih Tzu is longer than he is tall. He carries his tail curved over the back. The dog should have a broad, deep chest with firm shoulders and a level back. His legs are short but muscular. The movement of the Shih Tzu should be effortless and smooth-flowing. And the breed's characteristic mass of hair makes Shih Tzu look larger than they really are.

The Shih Tzu is described as a friendly, outgoing, trusting, and inquisitive breed. What's not to love in a dog with all these traits?

HAPPY PUP

The breed standard describes the ideal Shih Tzu as outgoing, happy, friendly, and affectionate. A well-bred Shih Tzu will adhere to the breed standard in both appearance and temperament. The best Shih Tzu doesn't just have proper breed characteristics, but also a pleasant and trusting personality.

Above all, pick a Shih Tzu that's right for you. The dog's playful and inquisitive nature may result in a few messes around the house, as he runs around under and behind furniture scouring the floor for hidden treasures. Keeping your Shih Tzu happy and well mannered are a part of your responsibility as an owner. Training a Shih Tzu can be humorous and a challenge, but with patience and the right training, your Shih Tzu is sure to be the best companion you ever have. To find a training class and other training resources once you've brought your new puppy home, search the AKC's extensive database for a training club in your area at www.akc.org /events/obedience/training_clubs.

At a Glance ...

The Shih Tzu is a Toy breed with a very distinct look. His floor-length coat and short-nosed "chrysanthemum face" are two of his outstanding physical traits.

· ·

The dog's small body should be muscular and well proportioned, longer than he is tall.

· ·

The Shih Tzu's gait should be smooth and flowing.

· ·

The breed's long body coat, head furnishings, and plumed tail are prized features, with the coat seen in a range of beautiful colors.

Finding Your Puppy

So you've decided to bring a Shih Tzu into your home? Great! Now it's time to go out and find one. Because the Shih Tzu is among the most popular dog breeds, you will have a selection of breeders to choose from who can help you select the best puppy for you. That means that you have hundreds of options, not all of which are equal, so it's important to start doing your homework on the breed early. Read up on the Shih Tzu as much as you can—in books, in magazines, and online. Then you'll know which

questions to ask breeders and which traits to look for when you start your puppy shopping. Be patient: it can sometimes take several months to find the perfect Shih Tzu puppy.

Breed clubs are a great source of help and information. Some even publish their own booklets about the breed, and they may publish a book of champions so that you can see what your puppy's famous ancestors actually looked like. There are also a number of specialized dog magazines geared toward pet dog owners and the show-dog world. You can find more information on these publications in the Resources section on page 122.

Bring any books or literature you've researched with you when you go puppy shopping. The Internet is also a wealth of breed information, but it's not always accurate. Anyone can set up a website and write what they like, regardless of their knowledge of the breed. The breed's parent club is a reliable source of information. The American Shih Tzu Club's website, www.americanshihtzuclub.org, has reliable information about the breed and offers links to other good sources of specific breed information.

Anyone with a love of the Shih Tzu can become a member of a breed club. The American Shih Tzu Club is the national club, but there are many regional clubs that are affiliated with the national club as well. In joining a club, you will meet other fanciers who share your interest in and preference for the Shih Tzu, and you can receive notification of Shih Tzu events in your area.

Because the Shih Tzu is one of America's most popular breeds, make sure you find an honest, reputable breeder to do business with. Set up an interview to meet with the person, examine the breeding facility, and meet the litter of puppies.

When you meet a breeder's dam (the mother of the litter), pay close attention to her temperament and personality. It's likely the pups will share some of these same characteristics.

CHOOSING A BREEDER

Responsible breeders breed their dogs for the sake of the breed, to maintain their bloodlines, rather than for money. To find a good breeder, browse the American Kennel Club and American Shih Tzu Club's online breeder directories. Talk to people at a dog show or other AKC-sponsored event, and ask them questions about their dogs. The more you familiarize yourself with the breed, the better equipped you'll be to find a great Shih Tzu.

While searching for the right breeder, look for one who fully understands the breed and has given careful thought to the way his Shih Tzu have been bred, taking into consideration the health and pedigrees of each dog in his breeding program.

The AKC recognizes good breeders through its Breeders of Merit program, which enrolls dedicated breeders who continue to produce healthy, capable, and beautiful purebred dogs. Each breeder in the program is required to have at least five years of involvement with AKC events and must have earned at least four titles for dogs that he has bred or co-bred. Breeders of Merit must also perform all required health screening as recommended by the breed's parent club, and they must ensure that all of their puppies are registered with the AKC. You can find a list of Breeders of Merit in your state through the AKC's website (www.akc .org/breederofmerit), as well as look up breeders with AKC litters on the site's online breeder classified listing.

Did You Know?

The Shih Tzu's long, silky coat is the breed's calling card. Pet Shih Tzu are usually trimmed so that their hair doesn't drag on the floor. All Shih Tzu, however, need to be groomed frequently to keep their coats vibrant and tangle-free.

Check the Contract

Most breeders have a puppy sales contract that includes specific health guarantees and reasonable return policies. The breeder should agree to accept a puppy back if things don't work out. He also should be willing to check up on the Shih Tzu's progress after the pup leaves for his new home and should be available to help if you have questions or problems with the pup.

If you're interested in getting a Shih Tzu as a companion, then any Breeder of Merit or other responsible breeder should be able to help you find a suitable pet. However, if you dream of walking your Shih Tzu into the show ring, then you will have to find a breeder who's willing to sell you one of his best dogs in order for you to compete in conformation.

Breeders are sometimes reluctant to sell their best dogs to novices unless the new owners demonstrate a serious desire to compete with their dogs. Keep in mind, too, that a show dog can cost more than a pet dog.

BE PATIENT

Once you've found a reputable breeder whom you would like to work with, chances are he probably won't have a puppy available the minute you want one. You may have to wait, especially if you are planning to buy a puppy with show

Make it Official

A responsible breeder will be able to provide your family with an American Kennel Club registration and pedigree.

AKC REGISTRATION: When you buy a new Shih Tzu puppy from a breeder, ask the breeder for an American Kennel Club Dog Registration Application form. The breeder will fill out most of the application for you. When you fill out your portion of the document and mail it to the AKC, you will receive a Registration Certificate certifying that your Shih Tzu is officially part of the AKC. Besides recording your name and your dog's name in the AKC registry, registration helps fund canine health research, search-and-rescue teams, public education about responsible dog care, and much more.

CERTIFIED PEDIGREE: A pedigree is an AKC certificate proving that your dog is a purebred Shih Tzu. It is your puppy's family tree, showing the names of his parents and grandparents. If your dog is registered with the AKC, the organization will have a copy of your dog's pedigree on file, which you can order from its website (www.akc.org). Look for any titles that your Shih Tzu's ancestors have won, including any AKC dog shows, competitions, or certifications. A pedigree doesn't guarantee the health or good personality of a dog, but it's a starting point for picking out a good Shih Tzu puppy.

Healthy, typical Shih Tzu will not be inexpensive. Many breeders may offer pet Shih Tzu at a lower price than show puppies, though you can't expect this. Since breeders often encounter one- or two-puppy litters, the expenses in breeding and rearing this breed is higher than with some others. The breeder of popular dogs such as Labrador Retrievers or German Shepherds can have eight to ten puppies in a litter. The demand for Shih Tzu keeps the price of puppies fairly high. Any well-bred puppy from a reputable breeder will be worth the price you pay, and good breeders are happy to sell their beloved puppies to good owners at a fair price.

potential. Even if you're just looking for a pet, you still have to wait at least ten to twelve weeks after a dam (mother) has given birth to and weaned her litter before they are ready to go to new homes.

Fortunately, there are many good breeders around. If you look carefully and know what to look for, you will find just such a person. If the breeder is personally referred by the breed's parent club, that is ideal, but you still need to be sure that the breeder's standards meet your expectations. The breeder you select will likely be someone who breeds from home, in which case the puppies have been brought up in the house and will be familiar with all of the activities and noises that surround them. For the socialization of the puppies, home rearing is ideal as the litter gets to meet people in the home and become accustomed to an ordinary home environment.

BREEDER SELECTION

Once you've found a few promising breeders who are responsible and trustworthy, follow these steps to help you make your final breeder selection:

STEP 1: Ask the Right Questions. Start your search by calling or e-mailing each breeder to ask some basic questions. Find out whether or not the breeders are involved in any American Kennel Club competitions or other dog-related activities. Breeders usually choose their winners from these competitions to breed their next litters of puppies. If the breeder has no competitive interest, you might want to keep looking for someone else to work with. Here are some other introductory questions to ask the breeder.

A good breeder's puppies will appear healthy, happy, and well groomed. Anything less than that is a sign to keep searching for another breeder.

• How long have you been breeding Shih Tzu? Breeders with ten or more years of experience are a plus.

• Have the puppies been raised in the home? These puppies tend to be better socialized and more easily looked after.

• Have you evaluated your litter for temperament? A good breeder will do everything possible to ensure his pups are ready to transition to a new home.

• How often is the mother bred? The answer should not be more than once a year. More often than that could signal an indiscriminate breeder.

• Do you have a purchase contract, and can I get all of your warranties and guarantees in writing? These answers should be *yes*! Don't just take the seller's word for it; a good breeder has no problem putting his guarantees in writing.

• Will you take the dog back any time, for any reason, if I can't keep him? A breeder who truly cares about his dogs will be willing to ensure them a good home whenever necessary.

STEP 2: Be Prepared to Answer Questions. Good breeders will ask you questions, too, so they can determine whether they want to do business with you. They will want to know about your previous experiences with dogs, your current home environment, and the reasons for your interest in the Shih Tzu. They are trying to determine whether you are the right fit for their puppies and if you will provide a good and loving home for whichever pup you choose. Common breeder interview questions may include the following.

- Have you previously owned a Shih Tzu? The breeder is trying to gauge whether you are already familiar with the breed and its specific needs. If this is your first Shih Tzu, don't worry—start sharing the information you have learned about the breed from your research. Your time spent reading about the breed will come in handy.

- How many hours are you away from home during the week? Shih Tzu can't just live in the backyard by themselves while you're at work. They need house-training and time away from the crate throughout the day. Let the breeder know that you understand the time commitment involved in owning a dog, and reassure him that you are excited and prepared for a Shih Tzu's daily care requirements.

- How long have you been interested in the Shih Tzu? Cautious breeders want to avoid impulse buyers. The breeder wants to hear that you have carefully thought through the decision before bringing a new dog home.

When you meet the pups, look for one with a sweet yet outgoing demeanor. Shy, anxious pups make for more difficult adults.

STEP 3: Visit the Breeder. If you feel that the initial interview went well, schedule a time to visit the breeder and the litter. Responsible breeders will welcome potential buyers so they can observe their home and facilities. While you're there, make note of whether the area is clean, if all dogs present appear healthy and well groomed, and if each pup has enough food and water and space to play. The breeder should also know each puppy by name and have an idea of each dog's personality. The dogs should all appear well socialized; fearfulness and anxiety are bad signs among dogs. Rather, the pups should be used to interacting with people and their littermates.

Don't plan multiple breeder visits back-to-back. Traveling from one litter to another can easily transmit bacteria, parasites, and diseases—dangers that young puppies may not be strong enough to fight against. Shower and change your clothes, including your shoes, each time you visit a breeder.

NARROWING THE SELECTION

However large or small the breeding establishment, it is important that the puppies are raised in suitable conditions. The areas should be clean, and the puppies should be well supervised in a warm, nurturing environment. The puppy you want should be

in tiptop condition and act like a happy little camper. Because Shih Tzu typically have two or three puppies in a litter, the selection in this breed will not be great. Nonetheless, the health and temperaments of all pups in the litter should be sound. The Shih Tzu is an outgoing breed, and this should be evident in the puppies' personalities. Look for a pup that is active and playful, rather than scared when you reach out to play with him.

The breeder should be perfectly willing to show you the litter's dam (mother); take careful note of her temperament and how she interacts with her offspring. If the dam is not available for you to see, this might be a sign that the puppy was not born on the premises but has been brought in from elsewhere to be sold. Inquire further about this.

As for the sire (father) of the litter, it is likely that he will not be on the premises and is owned by someone else. This is a common occurrence in dog breeding. A careful breeder may have traveled hundreds of miles to use a well-bred sire's stud services. Nonetheless, a dedicated breeder will at least be able to show you the sire's pedigree and a photograph of him, preferably winning a ribbon in the show ring!

When you review the pedigree, you will be fortunate if the pup's parents and grandparents have the title "Ch." in front of their names. It stands for "champion" conformation. Only top-quality Shih Tzu should be bred—yes, even if you're only seeking a pet dog.

WHAT TO LOOK FOR

All Shih Tzu puppies are appealing, but it is important to realize that this little bundle of furry fun will grow into a fully coated adult requiring time-consuming care and grooming. Bear this in mind before committing yourself to buying your new Shih Tzu pup. All puppies are cute, so don't just pick the first one you see. A good breeder will have checked that the puppy is in all-around good health before offering him for sale. Still, while selecting your puppy, look for the following signs. A healthy puppy should strike you as being clean, without any sign of discharge from the eyes or nose. His nose should be moist but not runny. Look for a round tummy that isn't swollen or potbellied. His rear end should be spotless, with no indication of diarrhea, which would be evident in a Shih Tzu's abundant coat. Although a puppy's nails can be sharp, they should not be too long, indicating that the breeder has clipped them as necessary.

The coat should be soft and shiny—in clearly excellent condition, without knots or tangles, rashes or missing hair. There should be absolutely no sign of parasites. The parasites themselves, such as fleas and lice, cannot always be seen easily, but a puppy's incessant scratching is a good pest indicator, and you might also notice a rash.

Scratching doesn't always indicate a parasitic or skin condition, though; it can also be associated with teething. In this case, the puppy will scratch only around his head. The puppy will stop doing this when his second set of teeth comes through and his gums are no longer sore.

Scratching might also be connected with an ear infection, so a quick look inside your new puppy's ears will ensure that there is no buildup of wax.

Crowd Control

All responsible dog owners who don't plan to breed their Shih Tzu should have them spayed or neutered. Female dogs are spayed, and males are neutered. Spaying or neutering has certain health benefits, such as reducing the chances of getting certain types of cancer. All owners of pet Shih Tzu should have their dogs spayed and neutered because it is the responsible thing to do.

In the right household and with the right dogs, sometimes two Shih Tzu are better than one. Take care to observe how they interact with each other and your family before comitting to the purchase.

There should be no odor from the ears, and they should be free of any redness or swelling.

Discuss hereditary diseases with your breeder. He should provide you with clearances for the conditions that affect the breed. According to the American Shih Tzu Club, screening requirements for the breed include progressive retinal atrophy (PRA), juvenile cataracts, entropion, renal dysplasia, thyroid disease, hip dysplasia, and von Willebrand's (hereditary bleeding) disease. Not all of these diseases affect all Shih Tzu, but conscientious breeders will never breed dogs that have not first been thoroughly screened and declared free of all disorders. You can ask to see written proof of the results, and remember to take note of the dates on which any tests were done.

The typical Shih Tzu temperament is friendly, so you can expect the same in a puppy. Don't take pity on the overly shy pup in the litter that hides away in a corner. Instead, search for a puppy that clearly enjoys your company when you visit; this will make for a long-term bond between the two of you. If possible, when you go to select your puppy, bring along the members of your household whom the puppy will also spend time with at home. It is essential that everyone agrees with the important decision you are about to make because a new puppy will inevitably change all of your lives.

NECESSARY PAPERWORK

A well-chosen breeder will be able to give new puppy owners lots of useful guidance, including advice about feeding, housing, and grooming. Make sure that the breeder you decide to work with has all of the essential paperwork and health verifications to accompany your purchase. Some thoughtful breeders give a small quantity of food to the new owners when the puppy leaves for his new home, as well as a blanket with the scent of his mother and littermates, which can comfort

your puppy during his first few days away from the breeder. In any event, the breeder should always provide written details of exactly what type and quantity of food should be fed, and with what regularity. At your discretion, feel free to change your pup's diet as time goes on, but make the change gradually to avoid stomach upset from the anxiety of so much change all at once.

The breeder will also need to tell you what vaccinations the puppy has received, if any. Details about the puppy's worming routine must also be provided. Gather any other relevant health documentation at the time of purchase. You should receive the puppy's pedigree, as well as the puppy's AKC registration papers which need to be filled out and mailed to the AKC or finished online at www.akc.org. Also ask for a sales receipt, health guarantee, and any documents to verify screening (the parents and the pup, where applicable) for health concerns in the breed. Some breeders also provide temporary insurance coverage for the puppy, which is a particularly nice bonus.

TAKE ADVICE

Listen to your breeder, a good one will do more than just breed cute puppies. He will also help you pick out the best puppy from his litter to fit your household and personality. If you're very serious about wanting to show your Shih Tzu, make sure your breeder knows. A show-bound puppy will cost more than a companion puppy. If the breeder is willing to sell you the puppy he considers to have the most promise, you must trust his judgment as he knows the litter and his line better than anyone. As long as you are honest with the breeder about your lifestyle, your intentions, and your dog experience, he will lead you to the right puppy.

At a Glance ...

With a popular breed like the Shih Tzu, there are many breeders out there. You will have to do your research to find a truly good one.

. . . .

A reputable breeder has experience with the Shih Tzu and chooses his breeding stock with care, giving great consideration to the health and pedigrees of the dogs in his breeding program.

. . . .

Make sure that your chosen litter (along with the areas in which the pups are kept) is the picture of health and cleanliness.

. . . .

The breeder should have sufficient knowledge of all breed-specific health problems and should be happy to show you health clearances for the parents, as well as proof of any testing done on the pups.

. . . .

Observe and interact with the litter to see which puppy's personality appeals to you most. Take the breeder's advice on this decision, as he will know each individual puppy best.

Welcoming the Shih Tzu

When the day arrives that your new Shih Tzu is ready to come home, you will want to be certain that everything at your house is as ready as it can possibly be. That means making sure that you have completed all puppy-proofing safety precautions and bought all necessary care equipment before your puppy arrives.

Most likely, you'll have had an opportunity to select and meet your puppy before the day

An exercise pen can be a great tool for containing your young puppy while house-training. Simply set your pup up in an uncarpeted room, wth food, water, and a blanket, and be sure to check on him for potty breaks throughout the day.

you bring him home from his breeder. Should this be the case, you will have had plenty of chances to discuss with the breeder exactly what your puppy will need to make life in his new home healthy, happy, and safe.

Depending on where you live, you probably have easy access to one of the large pet-supply stores or to a well-stocked privately owned shop. These stores carry basic supplies and a range of specialty items. Store owners and employees should be able help you pick out all you need for your new pup. Major dog shows

can be another great source for dog supplies; they often have vendor booths with products that cater to every doggie need, and you are sure to find more there than you ever dreamed of.

SHIH TZU SHOPPING LIST

Shopping for puppy supplies is a lot of fun, but it can get expensive, so start with the basics. Here's a list of all of the important goods your Shih Tzu will need.

Bedding: There's a dog bed out there for everyone. Dog beds come in every shape, size, and color—the choices are endless. But above all else, your Shih Tzu just needs one that is soft and a comfortable size for him to stretch out on. Don't go crazy and get the coolest, most expensive bed around. For example, wicker beds may look pretty, but they are dangerous, because puppies chew them. Sharp wicker pieces can all too easily injure eyes, get entangled in the Shih Tzu's coat or be swallowed. It's better to save your money until your Shih Tzu is older and less likely to chew up the fancy bed or soil it. While your puppy is still house-training, a large towel or blanket that can be washed easily will be plenty comfy—anything that will clean easily because it will certainly need to be washed a lot! If your pup will be sleeping in his crate, add a crate pad and place the blanket inside. Be sure to replace the padding and blanket as they become tattered. Check for any loose threads that your puppy's nails or teeth could get caught on because he is sure to play and chew on his bedding often.

Bowls: Your dog will need two bowls, one for food and one for water. Stainless steel or ceramic bowls are preferable because they are lightweight, chew-proof, and easy to clean. Plastics can retain bacterial microorganisms more easily, and some dogs develop plastic allergies, so some veterinarians recommend avoiding plastic bowls altogether. Because the Shih Tzu's face is flat, it's wise to purchase a bowl that is wider than it is deep to make feeding easier.

Collar and ID tag: Your Shih Tzu should have a collar that can expand to fit him as he grows. Lightweight, adjustable collars work best for both pups and adult dogs. You can place the collar on your new puppy for a few minutes at a time so he can get used to wearing it. The ID tag should have your dog's name and your cell phone number clearly displayed. In addition to the collar, owners should have their Shih Tzu microchipped, but the collar is the first line of protection to help a good neighbor return your dog if he ever gets lost.

Crate: A crate is the best tool for house-training your puppy, and it will become your Shih Tzu's favorite place to feel safe and protected. Think of it as your dog's special den. Crates come in different sizes, designs, and colors and are made of wire, fabric, or plastic. Because your Shih Tzu is a Toy breed, you won't need a very big crate for him; but make sure it is at least big enough for him to stand and move around in comfortably, even as he grows. Consider your puppy's estimated full-grown size when selecting his crate.

Gates: Baby gates are great to keep your puppy contained in certain parts or rooms of the house. It's a good idea to keep

String Danger

Some less obvious items that can hurt your puppy are dental floss, yarn, needles and thread, and other stringy things. Puppies exploring the house at ground level will find and swallow the tiniest of objects and can end up needing surgery. Most veterinarians will gladly tell you stories about the strange stuff they have removed from puppies' tummies.

your puppy in a tiled or uncarpeted room or space that has a door to the backyard for potty trips. It's much more difficult to clean potty accidents on carpeting, so avoid putting your pup in carpeted areas as much as possible. By keeping your puppy in a safe place where he can't get into trouble, you are helping him learn rules without causing too many problems around the house.

Exercise pen: An exercise pen is another great way to contain your tiny pup. The sturdy, self-enclosed pen provides a safe area where you can corral your Shih Tzu anywhere you like and have the ability to spend time with your pup in any location while still under a restricted, watchful eye. Be sure to place some newspapers or pee pads inside the pen with your pup for when he needs to go to the bathroom. Throw in a blanket and some safe toys to help keep him occupied.

Leashes: Buy two kinds of leashes: a thin, 6-foot leather or nylon leash and an extendable leash that lengthens and retracts with the push of a button. The shorter leash is best for house-training and teaching your puppy obedience lessons. The extendable leash is great to use when you are taking your Shih Tzu out on walks. It's a good idea to teach your puppy how to heel (walk beside you without pulling on the leash) before you use the extendable leash so that he doesn't get used to drifting too far from you on walks.

Puppy food: Your Shih Tzu will thrive on quality puppy food that is specially made for his age and size. Most dog foods have unique formulas for dogs of different sizes. Ask your breeder what food your puppy has been eating and get at least a couple of days' worth of that same food. To avoid an upset tummy, it's a good idea to keep your Shih Tzu eating the same food he's used to—after all, he will have more than enough changes to deal with. If you decide to change food brands, do so gradually over a few weeks by mixing more of the new formula with

the old each day until only the new food is in his bowl.

Toys: Puppies love to chew, so they need toys that are safe to gnaw on. If you don't give your Shih Tzu toys, he'll make chew toys out of other things around the house, like your shoes or furniture. Keep old shoes, socks, and slippers off-limits; even the smartest puppy can't tell the difference between his belongings and yours. Avoid tuggable toys for your Shih Tzu puppy; with such a little breed of puppy, that sort of toy can damage his teeth if pulled too hard. As soon as your puppy shreds his fuzzy toys, throw them away; you don't want your puppy to swallow any of the fuzz or choke on button eyes or plastic squeakers.

Before bringing your Shih Tzu puppy home, make sure you're fully stocked with everything he'll need for a stress-free transition from the breeder to his new home with you.

CLEANING SUPPLIES

These items are more for you than for your dog. You need to arm yourself with the right cleaning supplies before you bring your new puppy home. Until your Shih Tzu is house-trained, chances are you'll be cleaning up a lot of accidents. Keep lots of paper towels, old towels, and newspapers on hand for fast cleanups. And you'll need to invest in a strong enzymatic cleaner to remove any traces of urine that will otherwise draw your dog to the scene of the crime to pee again. It's instinct, so he won't be able to avoid it without your help.

GOOD GROOMING GETS

Because you have selected a long-coated breed, you will need various grooming tools, especially if you plan to show your Shih Tzu. Start with the basics, and as your dog matures and his coat becomes more demanding, add to your grooming tool kit. At this early stage, a soft bristle brush and high-quality comb will be your principal needs. Introduce your puppy to brushing as young as possible so that he learns to enjoy grooming time. It also will get your pup used to being handled, which will help when it's time to clean his teeth, clip his nails, or go to a groomer

HISTORICAL FACT

Many people mistakenly think Shih Tzu are Chinese dogs, but they were actually first bred by Tibetan monks and sent to the Chinese emperors from time to time as gifts. There is speculation that further breeding may have occurred at the Chinese court between Shih Tzu and Pekingese to produce the modern Shih Tzu we see today.

for a salon visit. You will also need to have dog shampoo on hand for bathing. Many Shih Tzu owners prefer to work on their dogs' coats on a grooming table. You can purchase a grooming table at a pet-supply store. Brushing your dog on the table is easier on your back and doubly useful for owners who will be competing with their dogs in conformation, as the table can be used to practice setting up your dog for the judging procedure.

For those necessary pedicures, you'll need pet-specific nail clippers. Don't try to use your own for the job. You can go high-tech or low; some clippers are equipped with sensors to detect where the nail's quick (vein) is, to avoid cutting too short and making your dog bleed. If you do accidentally cut the quick, use a styptic stick to stop the bleeding. Other grooming items you need include cotton balls (to clean your Shih Tzu's ears) and towels, both of which you probably already have in your home.

Dental cleaning from an early age will help fight oral disease later in life. Human-grade toothpaste is harmful to dogs, but you can get special toothpaste and brushes for dogs. The younger your Shih Tzu puppy is when you start brushing, the more tolerant of it he'll be as he grows.

ODDS AND ENDS

There are many other products that are great to have on hand when you first bring home your new puppy. Puppy pee pads can be a helpful potty-training tool while your Shih Tzu is learning where and when it's appropriate for him to go to relieve himself. They're also helpful for pet owners who might not be able to go home to let their puppies outside during the workday, or for those who live in apartments or places where taking your dog outside to go to the bathroom is inconvenient. While you're training your puppy, you'll also want to have some yummy treats at hand. There are many treat varieties available; just be sure to get something small enough for your tiny Shih Tzu pup to digest (or easy for you to break into pieces). Save the treats for special occasions, or you'll spoil his diet! And if you find that your positive-reinforcement training needs a little help to curb your puppy's teething frenzy, bitter apple-flavored sprays exist to aid in dogs' chewing-behavior modification.

PUPPY-PROOFING THE HOME

Although your Shih Tzu is small, remember that you have an active breed that can get into unimaginable mischief. That's why puppy-proofing your house is a must. If you don't, you will regret it—and so will your house!

Because your puppy is so low to the ground, it's important that

you check the floor for anything dangerous in every place he will have access to. Everyday household items may seem harmless, but something like a dainty cloth draped over the side of a little table full of fragile ornaments is merely asking for trouble! Even more dangerous to a mischievous puppy are electrical cords, so be sure they are tucked away well beyond your Shih Tzu's reach. Tiny teeth can bite through an electrical cord all too easily, causing a possibly fatal accident. Safely bundle up all electrical cords and hide them behind specially made covers.

Check your house for the following items that could be dangerous for your puppy, and place them out of his reach. The kitchen garbage can is a natural puppy magnet. Remember that your dog's nose is about 50,000 times more sensitive than yours. Just imagine how enticing these gross things smell to your new Shih Tzu puppy! Collect all medicine bottles, cleaning materials, and bug sprays from around the house and lock them up in a cabinet where your puppy can't get to them. Beware of fertilizers in your backyard and chemicals for cars like antifreeze and oil. These things are extremely toxic to your dog!

Another area you'll need to puppy-proof is your bedroom. Pick up clothes, books and important papers off the floor and put them in your hamper, in the closet, or on your desk—out of your Shih Tzu's reach. Don't forget to close your closet doors. Puppies love all of these things because they smell like their favorite person—you!

You'll be amazed at what your puppy will find around your home. That's why it's important to never let your puppy roam around your house unsupervised. Puppy-proofing is a never-ending chore. Your tiny, curious Shih Tzu will find his way into spaces that you thought he could never get into. You must always be a few steps ahead of him. Use common sense, and you and your Shih Tzu puppy will enjoy a happy and safe home life together.

Check around your floors to make sure that the only things available for your Shih Tzu to play with are the toys you *want* him to play with.

Store your dog's toys away somewhere easily accessible to you but out of your dog's reach. Rotate their use to keep the toys fun and new to your dog.

BEDTIME BASICS

Where you want your puppy to sleep will be a major consideration, and you should start off by putting him in his permanent sleeping area from the first night. It is only natural that the newcomer will be restless for the first couple of nights or so, but if you immediately take pity on your new pup and let him join you in your bed, he will expect to remain there always! And with a breed as small as the Shih Tzu, sharing your bed can be dangerous—you might accidentally roll over him in the middle of the night.

For the sake of safety, house-training and general care, a crate can also make a great puppy bedroom. A small wire crate serves the needs of the Shih Tzu perfectly. Inside the crate you will want to provide a nice soft pillow or crate mat, something easily washable because potty accidents in the puppy's crate must be expected for the first few weeks. In addition, you should give your puppy a small bed in which he can rest when he's spending time with the family. Choose a durable bed that can be washed or wiped down. It can easily be lined with comfortable, soft bedding that can be washed frequently. For your small Shih Tzu, choose a bed that is just slightly raised from the ground, or else position it away from drafts.

STAY HOME

You'll probably want to show off your new puppy to your friends the minute you bring him home. However, your puppy is making a big move in his short life, so the first two or three days are best spent quietly at home with you and your immediate family.

Once your puppy has become accustomed to his new surroundings, you will be able to introduce him to new people and places. Carefully supervise any time that young children spend with your little puppy. Youngsters are often attracted to the coat of a Shih Tzu, and little fingers can all too easily tug at the easily tangled coat and hurt the puppy, even with the most harmless intentions.

If your family has other pets, make introductions slowly and under careful supervision. Most Shih Tzu get along well with other animals, but you should still exercise caution. Because Shih Tzu think they are much bigger than they are, they do not fear larger dogs. Keep a close eye on interactions between your Shih Tzu and any other dog or animal, big or small.

GET SOCIAL

After your new puppy has completed all of his vaccinations and the veterinarian gives him the green light to explore the great outdoors and meet new people and dogs, it's your job to help him learn socialization. This is the most important part of a puppy's introduction to the human world. Although Shih Tzu are naturally outgoing and friendly, it is important to introduce them to strangers and new experiences at an early age. Pups that aren't socialized grow up to be scared and fearful of people and strange places. Some may become aggressive because of their fear and end up biting other dogs, strangers, or even you. Puppy socialization is the key to avoiding this and helping your new companion grow into a friendly, well-trained adult Shih Tzu.

The best time to socialize your dog is during his first twenty weeks of life. A good breeder will start the puppy's socialization process as soon as he's up and toddling about. The breeder will handle the puppy often, petting him and giving him lots of love—sometimes exposing him to people of all ages and encouraging them to handle the puppy, too. Litters raised in the breeder's home will become accustomed to the common sights, sounds, and smells around the house. Vacuum cleaners, coffee grinders, televisions and other noises can be frightening when puppies encounter them for the first time.

Once your Shih Tzu leaves the safety of his mother and littermates at around ten weeks of age, it's your job to continue his socialization training. Start with a quiet house for the first few days, letting him get used to his new environment, then slowly introduce him to the sights and sounds of his new world. Visit new places (dog friendly, of course) like parks or the common area of an outside shopping center where there are crowds of people. Take him to the pet store and pet-friendly restaurants. Introduce him to people from all walks of life: adults and children, males and females, people in uniforms, people in wheelchairs, people with beards and mustaches, and all different ethnicities.

Familiarize your puppy to as many new situations and people as you can, so he won't be afraid of the encounter later in life. Set a goal to visit two new places

Get Low

The best way to puppy-proof any room is to get down on all fours; that way, you see the room from your Shih Tzu's perspective. You never know what dangerous things you might find this way. For example, a stray rubber band or a half-eaten candy bar hidden under the couch. These things can be very dangerous, so make sure to "crawl" around to complete your puppy-proofing sweep of the house.

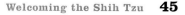

a week for the next few months. Keep all of these situations upbeat and positive, which will teach your puppy that new experiences are happy and exciting.

While he's still young, take your Shih Tzu to puppy school. Some classes accept pups from ten to twelve weeks of age, as long as your puppy has had all of his shots. The younger the pup, the easier it is to train him. A good puppy class will teach good behavior rather than just obedience skills. Your puppy will be able to meet and play with other young dogs, and you will learn what tools you will need to train your puppy. Peer interaction is important to help avoid or diminish any fear or anxiety your pup might have toward other dogs. Consistency and positivity are key in early socialization and training.

Puppy classes are important both for your dog and for you—especially if this is your first dog. Be a smart Shih Tzu owner; continue with your dog studies and take more advanced training classes together as your pup gets older. Just like you, your puppy needs all the education he can get!

Once your Shih Tzu has had all his shots and has acclimated to his new home, take him on various outings to meet new people and see new places. It's the first step in important lifelong training.

At a Glance ...

Take the breeder's advice about what you will need for your new puppy and have these items on hand prior to the puppy's arrival.

· ·

Make a list of all the important products you will need for your Shih Tzu, and take it with you when you go on your pre-puppy shopping spree.

· ·

Pick a location for your pup's sleeping area and get into a bedtime routine. Don't give in to your Shih Tzu's whining during those first few nights; in due time, he will settle down.

· ·

Puppy-proofing is a must! Remember that pups are curious little creatures and you don't want them to explore their way into danger.

· ·

Introductions to all family members, including other pets, should be done with care so as not to overwhelm the pup with too much too soon.

ShihTzu Training Time

When your young Shih Tzu puppy first arrives home, give him some time to get used to his new surroundings and housemates. Because the Shih Tzu has a friendly nature and is a true "people person," the socialization process should happen quite easily, but don't overwhelm him with too many new faces, sounds, and smells all at the same time! Before you know it, you will be able to introduce your puppy to people outside the

family. Give him time to adjust and become comfortable in his new home. Then, it's time for training lessons.

THE LEADER OF THE PACK

All dogs need someone to lead them. Your Shih Tzu's dam (mother) was the first to take charge, watching over him and his brothers and sisters when he was first born. When he played too rough, his littermates cried and stopped the game. When he got too pushy, his mom shook him gently by the scruff of the neck.

Remember, human rules don't make sense to your puppy. You must direct him in how to interact in the human world and help him understand what's right and wrong. This isn't easy, but it will strengthen your relationship with your pup.

The first five months of your Shih Tzu's life is the most important learning time for him. His mind is able to absorb more training lessons than at any other time in his life. You must fill this part of your puppy's life with positive training and introduce him to different types of people and places. This is called socialization, and it will help your puppy grow into a well-behaved, friendly dog. Socialization shows your puppy that strangers and new places aren't scary or dangerous.

THE WAITING GAME

Depending on the age of your puppy and whether his course of vaccinations is complete, you may or may not be able to take him out in public places right away.

Make Your Puppy a S.T.A.R.

The American Kennel Club has a great program for new puppy owners called the S.T.A.R. Puppy Program, which is dedicated to rewarding puppies that get off to a good start by completing a basic training class. S.T.A.R. stands for: Socialization, Training, Activity, and Responsibility.

You must enroll in a six-week puppy training course with an AKC-approved evaluator. When the class is finished, the evaluator will test your puppy on all the training taught during the course, such as being free of aggression toward people and other puppies in the class, tolerating a collar or body harness, allowing his owner to take away a treat or toy, and sitting and coming on command.

If your puppy passes the test, he will receive a certificate and a medal. You and your puppy will also be listed in the AKC S.T.A.R. Puppy records. To learn more about the AKC S.T.A.R. Puppy Program or to find an approved evaluator near you, check out www.akc.org/starpuppy.

Once your puppy comes of age, introduce him to people in your neighborhood in a fun, relaxing environment.

Either way, it's probably best to let him settle in at home for the first few days before venturing into the big wide world. There is still lots you can do with your Shih Tzu puppy, so you will both undoubtedly have great fun, but remember that his tiny little body needs sufficient rest time, too.

If restricted to your home for a little while, you can play games together with safe, soft puppy toys. Do not let your pup tug on his toys, as you do not want to cause chaos to his delicate young tooth formation; this is an extra concern for breeds with undershot jaw lines like the Shih Tzu. Your puppy's teeth will be very sharp and able to damage toys. Check his toys regularly for sharp or unsafe parts, such as plastic eyes or squeaker parts that could become detached. These small pieces are choking hazards and can cause injury to a puppy's teeth and mouth.

Put your time together at home to good use, preparing your puppy for training and other experiences to come. Introduce your Shih Tzu to standing calmly on a table and lying on his side to be gently groomed. Both will be helpful on numerous occasions, including visits to the veterinarian, where it is much easier to deal with a well-behaved dog. Plus, you will be so proud of your clever and polite companion!

CRATE INTRODUCTION

Whether you have a show dog or a house pet, you will need to train your puppy to stay in a crate when required; chances are your Shih Tzu is going to spend time in one at some point or another. In the home, most dogs consider the crate as a safe place to retreat to when necessary and don't mind staying there for short periods

Did You Know?

Although few breeds are further in appearance from wild dogs, the Shih Tzu is one of the closest-related breeds of dogs to wolves. DNA studies confirm that the Shih Tzu is one of fourteen ancient breeds, including the Chow Chow, Tibetan Terrier, Lhasa Apso, and Chinese Shar-Pei.

of time, which can be helpful when you can't be home to watch over your pup 24/7. For all dogs, crates are useful and safe for travel.

When you start crate-training, remain within your Shih Tzu's eyeline and give him a toy or treat to occupy his mind while he gets used to the restriction. Leave your pup in the crate for very short intervals of time—just a minute or two at first, then gradually build up the duration. Never confine a puppy to a crate for long periods of time. As he grows, he'll be able to stay in his crate longer. Many dogs adapt to sleeping in their crates overnight.

TAKE THE LEAD

Before you embark on training lessons, you'll need to get your puppy used to being on a lead; it's always a strange

Training Tips

Successful puppy training depends on several important principles:

1. Use simple one-word commands and say them only once. Otherwise, your Shih Tzu will learn that "Come" (or "Sit" or "Down") is a three- or four-word command.

2. Never correct your dog for something he did a few minutes earlier. He won't remember what he did wrong. Correct him in the act.

3. Always praise (and offer a treat) as soon as he does something good (or when he stops doing something bad). How else will your Shih Tzu know he's a good dog?

4. Be consistent. You can't play on the bed together today, but then tell him it's wrong to cavort on the bed tomorrow.

5. Never call your dog to you to correct him. He won't want to come when called because he thinks he may be in trouble. Always go to your Shih Tzu to correct bad behavior, but be sure you catch him while he is doing something wrong, or he won't understand why he is in trouble.

6. Never, *ever* hit your dog as punishment. Nothing could be more damaging to your relationship with your Shih Tzu than a physical correction. Hitting your dog will only make him afraid and distrustful of you, and he may react by growling or biting. Be sure to only use your voice to correct your Shih Tzu, and keep your paws to yourself!

7. When you are rewarding your dog or correcting him, be sure to let your voice do the talking.

8. Use a light, happy voice when your Shih Tzu does something good and a calm, firm voice when your dog does something wrong. Remember that your Shih Tzu doesn't speak English any more than you speak Tibetan, but he can understand the tone of your voice.

experience for a young pup. Start by attaching a simple collar, not too tight to choke or too loose to catch on surrounding objects and cause panic and possible injury. Put the collar on for a few minutes at a time at first, lengthening the duration slightly until your puppy feels comfortable with it on, which may take a few days.

Once your Shih Tzu is comfortable in his collar, attach a small lightweight lead. Select one with a secure catch that is still simple enough to attach and release as necessary. Until now, your puppy has gone wherever he pleased; he will find it very strange to be attached to someone who is restricting his movements. To ease the process, let your Shih Tzu lead you for the first few sessions on the lead. Start to exert a little pressure at a time, and your puppy will effortlessly tag along with you as you lead the way. That's when you'll be ready to start the real training.

REWARDING AND CORRECTING

Dogs respond best to positive reinforcement. Just as we are more inclined to repeat a behavior if we receive a positive response, the same is true for your Shih Tzu. Dogs' behavior tells us that anything a dog does that is rewarded will be repeated. This is called positive reinforcement. If something good happens when a dog does something, like receiving a tasty treat or hugs and kisses, he will want to do it again. So be sure to have lots of dog treats in your pockets when training

Puppy training classes are a great place to teach your dog proper social interaction with other dogs and with you.

your Shih Tzu. The easiest way to let your pup know he did something right is to give him a treat!

But what do you do when your dog does something wrong? Never shout or get angry at your Shih Tzu; with a breed as sensitive and intelligent as this one, it will do more harm than good. Try to use the same training idea, but instead of a treat, correct the dog by saying a word like "no" in a calm voice and moving him away from what he is doing wrong. It is important to catch your dog while he is doing something wrong because, if you correct him later, he won't understand what he did wrong.

Get Good Training Help

Here are suggestions for finding training professionals who are compatible with your philosophies and needs:

- Be clear about the kind of training you want for your dog. It helps to know this ahead of time, before you start shopping for trainers. Read training books and research online. Choose the philosophies that meet your needs.

- Locate trainers in your area. Look online and ask your dog-owning friends, veterinarian, and breeder for any referrals. The Association of Pet Dog Trainers promotes dog-friendly training methods, and many of the organization's members are postive-method trainers. You can find a list of APDT member trainers in your area by searching their site, www.apdt.com.

- Interview potential trainers who you're interested in. Be certain that their techniques, training methods, and services offered meet your training goals.

- Observe a class. If a potential trainer says no to this request, then move on to someone else. Watch the trainer at work to be sure you are comfortable with the training methods and style.

- Ask for references. Contact past students to find out about their experiences in class.

- Select the trainer you are most comfortable with, and sign up! Keep in mind that you can leave and go to another trainer at any time, if you become uncomfortable or disagree with anything the trainer does. Your Shih Tzu's safety and well-being are the most important factors.

KEYS TO SUCCESS

There are a few things that you need to know before you start training your Shih Tzu. Remember that you need to be your dog's leader. Let him know that you are in charge. You'll have to teach him in a way that he will understand. Your puppy doesn't understand human rules, so be patient. It will take time for your Shih Tzu to understand what you're trying to teach him—and for you to understand him.

Repeat, repeat, repeat: Use the same word or cue for each behavior every time you teach it, adding treats and lots of verbal praise such as "Good dog!" and clapping to let your puppy know when he does something correctly. After a few times, your Shih Tzu will understand and will be excited to repeat the behavior when he hears that same training word. For example, when teaching your pup to go potty outside, use the same potty words ("Go potty," "Get busy," or "Hurry up") each time he goes, adding the praise "Good boy!" when he's done. Your dog will soon learn the correct reasons for those trips outside.

Keep it short and sweet: Timing is important when training your puppy. You have to catch him at the exact moment he is doing something good or bad to teach him whether something is right or wrong. If you correct your Shih Tzu more than five seconds after he's done something wrong, he won't understand

Take Charge

Wild dogs live in groups called "packs." In these packs, one dog acts as the leader and all the other dogs follow him and learn from him. As a canine, your Shih Tzu still needs to have a leader. By training your dog when he is a puppy, he will learn from you as he would from his pack leader.

In potty training—as in all dog training—patience and repetition are key. Be sure to use the same cue words whenever you take your pup outside to relieve himself.

why he's in trouble. So be sure to stay close to your pup and watch him carefully; you want to be ready to train him the moment he does anything good or bad.

CLICKER TRAINING

The clicker method of positive-reinforcement training has fast become popular among dog trainers and pet owners alike. It has been widely used by animal trainers for decades and been made more available to the general public in recent years with the arrival of many clicker training-related products on pet store shelves.

In clicker training, the trainer uses a tool called the "clicker," typically a small plastic box with a metal tongue that makes a clicking sound when it is pressed. This click sound is used to mark the exact instant of a desired behavior, which the trainer then follows with an immediate reward such as praise or a small treat. The closer the reward happens in time to the behavior, the faster the pup makes the connection and understands what he must do to earn another reward. Shih Tzu aim to please and are very responsive to positive training techniques. Clicker training is easy—just follow these simple guidelines.

Begin by charging the clicker, teaching your dog that a reward is coming every time he hears the marker sound. Click and treat about a dozen times in rapid succession. At this point, the goal is to simply teach your puppy to associate the clicking noise with the treat. You'll know the clicker is charged when you see your Shih Tzu's eyes light up when he hears the click, then looks to you for a reward. You can use other markers besides the clicker, as well, such as a tongue cluck or a short and distinct marker word.

Now you're ready to apply the charged clicker's usefulness as a tool in whatever you want to train your dog to do. For instance, lure your puppy into a sit position. Say "Sit" and click the clicker just as your Shih Tzu's hind end hits the floor. Then immediately give him a treat. Repeat this multiple times in a row, and your well-trained puppy will soon know just what to do the moment you tell him to "Sit."

Start training young, and your Shih Tzu will grow to be a well-mannered and pleasant adult.

At a Glance ...

Allow your pup to get used to his home and surroundings and to bond with everyone in the family.

....

Once your Shih Tzu puppy is safely vaccinated, you can begin to introduce him to the big world beyond your house.

....

Engage your puppy in games with his toys to keep him occupied and active at home.

....

Accustom your Shih Tzu to gentle brushing on your lap or a grooming table.

....

Let your pup wear his leash and collar to get used to it, and begin a little informal leash training.

....

Introduce your Shih Tzu to a crate in a happy manner. The crate will be your most valuable training and safety aid.

....

Clicker training is an effective and easy form of positive-reinforcement pet training.

CHAPTER SIX

Help for House-Training

For every dog owner, house-training is one of the most important things that your new dog must learn. House-training can be difficult to accomplish with your Shih Tzu. However, with patience, positive reinforcement, and keen attention to your pup's feeding schedule and behavior, it can be done—provided that you are consistent in your approach. To house-train with success, you will need to be firm but never harsh, and you must never be rough with

Watch the Water Intake

Pick up your puppy's water bowl after 7 p.m. This will help your puppy from having to go to the bathroom so much at night. If he gets thirsty, offer him an ice cube. Most Shih Tzu love ice, and your puppy will soon come running every time he hears the ice machine rattle in the kitchen.

ASSESS YOUR PUPPY'S TRAINING NEEDS

When your puppy first arrives in your home, depending on his age and experience he may or may not already be house-trained. However, you must remember that your home is completely different from his previous surroundings, so he will have to relearn the house rules. Doors and hallways are in new, unfamiliar places, and your family may go to bed and rise at different times than your new dog is used to, so it will undoubtedly take him time to learn and to adapt.

The speed of house-training success depends to a certain extent on your living environment and the season of the year. Most puppies are perfectly happy to go out into the yard in dry weather, but when it is raining (or even snowing!), most will need considerable positive encouragement!

FIRST IMPRESSIONS

One of the first things you should do when you bring your new Shih Tzu home is introduce him to his new crate. Do not force him inside the crate right away. Instead, toss a few treats inside the crate and encourage him to explore it on his own. Every time he enters the crate, say a cue word such as "Inside" or "Crate," and be sure to use this same word every time he enters the crate so that he will learn that this cue means to go inside his crate. Praise him and give him a treat whenever he goes inside the crate on his own. Soon, he'll learn that his crate is a happy, positive, and fun place.

On his first night home, your Shih Tzu puppy should sleep in his crate. Don't give in to his whines and cries. If you succumb and let him sleep in your bed, he'll

Hard as his adorable little face is to resist, it's best to train your Shih Tzu pup to sleep in a crate on his own from the first night he arrives.

learn that crying and whining will be rewarded with what he wants—a spot right next to you in bed! If you let your dog sleep in your bed, he'll start to think that he is the leader, and it will be harder to train him for the rest of his life. Hold strong against his whimpering; he'll soon settle down and go to sleep. After the first few nights, he'll learn that his crate is his own comfy bed, not yours!

Make your puppy's crate more comfortable by placing it near your bed. Your puppy will hear you nearby and feel reassured by your presence. You can also try placing one of your unlaundered T-shirts in the crate with your pup so that he can snuggle with it. Because it smells like you, he will feel safer and more relaxed.

CRATE TRAINING

Crate training is the most effective and popular method of house-training. It is based on a simple canine precept: dogs don't soil their sleeping areas. Your Shih Tzu is a classy Tibetan tyke and, of course, relishes clean bedding. This is true of not only your elegant Toy dog but all dogs—purebreds and mutts alike! Instinctually, all dogs want to keep their sleeping areas clean. The crate serves as the dog's sleeping area, and therefore the dog will make every effort to keep his crate clean.

During the day, your Shih Tzu will use his crate for naps and playtime. Some trainers recommend feeding the dog in the crate so that he associates it with happy times, but keep your potty-training goals in mind. The more food you give your Shih Tzu, the more he will have to go to the bathroom!

Put your puppy in his crate whenever you are not around to watch him closely. It will become a place for naps, at night, and whenever you need some time to run errands or leave the house for short periods of time. Don't worry, he will let you know when he needs to go to the bathroom.

Walk This Way

Don't carry your Shih Tzu to his potty area. Instead, lead him there on a leash or encourage him to follow you on his own if the designated area is safely enclosed. Although your Shih Tzu's small size makes it tempting to simply carry him around everywhere, if you start carrying your puppy to go to the bathroom, he might associate it as part of the routine. You may end up stuck in this routine for a long time, and your Shih Tzu will have trained you instead.

Dog Meet Crate

Your Shih Tzu breeder may have introduced your puppy to a crate already, but it's more likely that your pup has never seen a crate. It's up to you to make sure that his first experiences with a crate are positive and fun. Your puppy will come to love his crate in no time!

Every time you release your puppy from his crate, bring him outside to his potty area (or to the newspaper, if you live in a high-rise apartment or don't have a convenient outdoor area). Be sure to always take him to the same potty area and use the same house-training cues—repetition is the key to your puppy's understanding. Simple cues are very helpful: "Go potty" or "Get busy" are two popular choices. Any phrase will work, but be sure to repeat, repeat, repeat so that your puppy will start to learn what you want him to do. Praise him by getting excited, clapping your hands, and showering him saying "Good dog!" and giving lots of pets and rubs every time he goes to the bathroom correctly. He'll begin to understand when and where you want him to go potty, and he will want to please you again and again.

CRATE LIMITS

Your Shih Tzu's crate is one of the most valuable training tools that you have, but be sure not to keep your dog inside it for too long. Shih Tzu puppies under twelve weeks of age should not be kept in a crate for longer than two hours at a time—unless it is nighttime and they are sleeping, of course! For three- to five-month-old puppies, it's best not to keep them in their crate for longer than three to four hours. For dogs older than six months, limit crate time to six hours at a time. If you or someone in your household can't come home during the day to take your Shih Tzu out of his crate for a potty break and walk, try finding a dog walker or neighbor to come by and check on him.

Newspaper and pee pad training are not preferred potty training methods, but they'll do in a pinch or if you plan to continue this house-training technique for the duration of your dog's life.

Your Shih Tzu's crate will become a safe haven for your new pup. Be sure to keep all of your Shih Tzu's experiences with his crate positive and fun. Never use your dog's crate for punishment. The crate should be a comfortable and warm place where your dog enjoys spending time. If your puppy sees the crate as a negative place where he goes when he is bad, he will think that he is in trouble whenever you put him inside.

But what if you need to put him in his crate while you clean up a mess he has just made in the house? Yes, you can do this, but just don't be angry or say "bad dog" when you put him inside. He should never associate the crate with something bad or uncomfortable.

PAPER TRAINING

Paper training is always useful in the very early stages of training when your puppy is very young. However, most dog trainers agree that paper training your dog, and then retraining him to eliminate outside can be very confusing for your pet. However, paper training may be the only choice if you live in a city high-rise or are unable to take your dog outside regularly.

When paper training, place a few layers of paper (or a specially designed pee pad) by the door that you normally use to venture outside so that the pup learns

Life Outside the Crate

If you prefer not to use a crate, what can you do with your puppy when you're not home? Use baby gates to close off an area of your house, and place your puppy in this area when you need to leave him alone. Puppy-proof the area by removing anything he can chew on or hurt himself with. Even in a puppy-proofed area, some Shih Tzu pups will chew through walls or drywall if they are bored. You can also buy a small exercise pen from a local pet store that is about 4-by-4-feet square. This sturdy pen will provide a safe area where you can leave your dog for a short time if you need to. Remember to place some newspapers or pee pads in the area for your dog if he needs to go to the bathroom; also, include a blanket and some safe chew toys to keep him comfortable and happy while you're gone.

A PIECE OF HISTORY

Records of the first Shih Tzu in the United States date back to the 1940s and '50s, when they accompanied returning American soldiers home from war.

to associate the paper with the exit to the outdoors. Whenever your Shih Tzu uses the paper, he should be praised. Obviously, it is ideal if the puppy can be taken outside as soon as he shows any sign of wanting to do his business, but again this may depend on whether your home has immediate access to an outside area. If your puppy is having a hard time understanding what the paper is for, use a sponge to place a bit of his urine on the paper to draw him to the scent. This may encourage him to go to the bathroom in the right spot.

LOTS AND LOTS OF TRIPS OUTSIDE

Remember that puppies need to go potty much more frequently than adult dogs, especially after eating and sleeping. Be sure to take your puppy outside to potty after every playtime, feeding, and nap time. In fact, if you can, take your pup outside every hour while he is awake. Always keep your eyes and ears open because a puppy will not be able to wait those extra two or three minutes until it is convenient for you to let him out. You must be vigilant! If you delay, accidents will certainly happen. Half of your day will be spent leading your Shih Tzu outside for his potty trips. Welcome to dog ownership—it's not all glamour owning a Shih Tzu.

As your puppy matures and house-training sets in, asking to be let out when necessary will become second nature to your dog, and it is rare to encounter a Shih Tzu that is unclean in the house. Be patient and consistent, and soon your puppy will be a perfectly well-mannered, potty-trained pup.

Be prepared to spend half of your time with your new puppy taking him outside to relieve himself and the other half of your time feeding, cleaning, and preparing to take him back outside.

Home-Cleaning Solutions

Use these quick tips to keep your home clean while house-training your puppy.

• **If you don't have any professional cleaners on hand, create your own using ¼ cup of white vinegar to 1 quart of water.**

• **Salt will absorb fresh urine and remove some of the scent.**

• **In a pinch, rubbing the area with a dryer sheet can remove some of the odor.**

• **White toothpaste can sometimes remove some tough stains from carpet. But beware: it may ruin the carpet's coloring! Never use toothpaste on dark-colored carpets.**

BE FORGIVING

When accidents happen (and a lot of accidents will happen), give a verbal reprimand, but only if you catch your Shih Tzu in the act. Don't scold him after the event because he will simply not understand what he has done wrong, and this will only serve to confuse him.

The key is to catch him in the act. When you see your Shih Tzu going to the bathroom in the house, clap your hands loudly and give a verbal reprimand such as "No" or simply "Aaah! Aaah!" The sound of your voice should startle the pup. Immediately pick him up and take him outside to his potty place. Once he finishes going potty in the right spot, praise him with lots of pets and positive encouragements. If you are too late and your Shih Tzu has already gone potty in the house, simply clean up the mess and be more watchful of your pup. Sniffing the carpet and circling the floor are sure signs that your pup is looking for a spot to go. Vow to catch him the next time and make it a positive learning experience,

ACCIDENT CLEANUP

When cleaning up your Shih Tzu's accidents, be sure to clean the area thoroughly right away because your dog will be able to smell the remains of the accident and will be tempted to go to the bathroom in the same spot again. In order to clean up the entire accident and leave no trace behind, there is a technique to use when removing stains and odors from your floors.

If your dog urinates on the carpet, first take an old towel and soak up as much of the liquid as you can. Then, use an enzyme-based cleanser (but never anything that is pine-based, as it can be harmful to dogs and cats) and douse the area. Let the cleanser sit and break down the chemicals in the urine. This will

Time to Go!

Part of house-training is being able to read your puppy's potty cues before he has an accident. All dogs have different ways of telling you when they need to go. Some bark or run to the door, while others subtly twitch or stare off into space.

If you want to skip these signals altogether, you can try teaching your Shih Tzu to ring a bell when he wants to go outside. To teach this trick, hang a bell on the doorknob or the wall next to the door that you always use to go to your dog's potty area. Make sure the bell is within your puppy's reach; you'll have to hang it pretty low for your Toy dog to reach it. Every time you take him on a potty run, ring the bell before you walk out the door. Eventually, your Shih Tzu will make the connection and start ringing the bell on his own. When he does, praise him and take him outside. The positive reinforcement will stick, and soon your pup's potty cues will be clear as a bell.

not only clean the stain from the carpet, but it will also clear the scent from the area so that your dog will not be drawn to the same spot to relieve himself. White vinegar can act as a cleanser as well, but be sure not to use ammonia-based cleansers because ammonia is a component in urine and will simply strengthen the scent.

After the area has been doused with cleanser, press a clean towel into the spot to soak up the excess cleanser. Place a heavy item like a book or a weight on top of the towel to draw out any additional, leftover moisture. Once the spot is dry, remove the towel and sprinkle baking power over the area. Then vacuum to remove any trace of smell or moisture.

For accidents that involve solid waste, use toilet paper to pick up as much of the stool as possible and flush it down the toilet. Then douse the spot with cleanser and follow the same steps for cleaning up urine accidents. Though it is a long process, this is the best way to clean up accidents as they happen to keep your house clean and your puppy on track. Until your Shih Tzu is fully potty-trained, it's also a good idea to get your carpets professionally cleaned regularly to remove any hidden spots you may have missed.

House-training can be a challenging obstacle for your Shih Tzu. Be patient and consistent, and above all, stay positive! Before you know it, your pup will be potty-trained and your home will be accident free.

At a Glance ...

The first step on the road to a happy existence with your Shih Tzu is to teach him positive house-training habits.

. . . .

Paper training can help if you live in a high-rise or in a home with little access to an outside area, but this method is not as reliable as crate-training for a long-term solution.

. . . .

Be sure that your Shih Tzu's association with his crate is a positive one. Many dogs learn to love their crates and choose to spend time there on their own.

. . . .

Puppies require many bathroom trips each day! Be sure to praise your Shih Tzu when he goes in the right place; reprimand him for accidents only if you catch him in the act.

. . . .

Choose a bathroom cue and be consistent with your schedule and training. Soon your pup will learn to let you know when it's time for a potty break.

CHAPTER SEVEN

Teaching Basic Commands

Shih Tzu are ready learners, but they can sometimes be stubborn in their own cute way. Owners, often completely enraptured by their Shih Tzu's near human-like behavior and intelligence, allow their dogs to misbehave, which is not a good thing for human or dog. For all Shih Tzu, obedience training is a must, as it makes your companion more reliable and enjoyable in the home. All dogs who accompany their owners in public, whether it's to the dog park for a romp,

a nursing home to visit patients, or just down the street for a walk, must exhibit good manners and basic obedience. There's no excuse for a dog's bad behavior, whether he's a 9-pound Shih Tzu or a 200-pound Mastiff.

THE NAME GAME

First and foremost, your new Shih Tzu puppy must learn his name. With a pocket full of treats, teaching your dog his name is a simple and fun first lesson during which you will bond with your new pup. Be careful not to overfeed him during your training sessions—you don't want to end up with a pudgy puppy. Use small, soft treats that are easy to chew such as cut up hot dogs or unsalted, plain popcorn. These treats are delicious and nutritious for your Shih Tzu.

When teaching your dog his name, call your Shih Tzu just once and wait for him to respond. If you repeat his name over and over, he will begin to think that the repetition is part of his name. Simply say his name once, and when he responds, quickly toss him a treat. Do this at least a dozen times, several times a day. Over a few days, you'll start to notice that he will begin to respond to his name right away in anticipation of a treat. This name game not only teaches your new puppy his name but also helps call his attention to you. It is important to be able to keep and hold your dog's attention when you are training him. What better way to hold his attention than with a yummy treat!

TRAINING TIPS

Get started on the right foot with these suggestions for making training sessions easier and more productive.

1. **Quiet, Please.** A new puppy is easily distracted. Pick a quiet place to train your pup—no TV, music, animals, or other people nearby. Don't give your Shih Tzu puppy an excuse not to have his full attention on you. Once you teach a simple cue such as sit, and you feel that your Shih Tzu has it down pat, try bringing your puppy into a place with another person or animal in the room. If your puppy hesitates or doesn't react to the cue because his attention is elsewhere, take him back to the quiet place and train him a little more. If your puppy can sit on cue with no hesitation even with distractions, you are right on track!

2. **One on One.** Keep it simple. In the beginning, have only one person train your puppy. At this stage, your pup will get confused if more than one person is telling him what to do. It's important that your Shih Tzu recognize only one person as the leader at first. Otherwise, he won't know which way to look when he is called! Once your puppy knows his cues well, try introducing other members of your family into the training process.

3. **Keep It Short.** Don't ask too much of your pup right away. Keep your lessons short and simple. The key to training is to keep it fun and exciting. As soon as you've lost your puppy's attention, all of your training efforts are in vain. When your Shih Tzu starts looking around and won't respond when you say his name, it's time to stop. Come back to the lesson the next day, and try to change it slightly so that each training session is new and fresh.

4. **Always Praise.** Dogs respond well to positive-reinforcement training. In other words, get excited when you train your pup and shower him with praise and belly rubs. Don't try to train when you are grumpy. If you're feeling frustrated or angry, you will convey your feelings to your Shih Tzu, and the whole training experience will become somber and negative. Above all things, your dog wants to please you, so show your Shih Tzu that he makes you happy through lots of praise and treats.

5. **End Positively.** Make sure to end every lesson positively, with a reward and lots of praise. If your Shih Tzu is having a hard time sitting on cue, but he always comes to you when called, have him run, and call him back to you at the end of the lesson. Deliver a big treat and a warm hug, showing him that you are proud of all he has accomplished.

Attention-Seeking Behavior

Before you begin a training lesson, pretend to ignore your Shih Tzu puppy for a few minutes. This will make your dog want your attention even more. By the time you do give your pup attention for a quick training session, he will be really eager for your company and will be willing to listen to what you say. Perfect!

CUE UP

In all training, it is essential to get your dog's full attention, which many owners do with the aid of treats so that the dog learns to associate treats with praise and desired behaviors. The following training methods involve food treats, but eventually you will wean your dog off these training aids and focus instead on praise and petting as rewards. Always use very simple cues, just one or two short words, and keep sessions short so they do not become boring for your dog.

TAKE IT, LEAVE IT, DROP IT

The *take it* and *leave it* cues are two of the first lessons that you will teach your Shih Tzu. These two lessons show your pup that you are the leader and will help him understand that you know what's best for him. To teach the *take it* cue, place a treat in the palm of your hand and hold it in front of your Shih Tzu. As the dog takes the treat, say "Take it." After repeating this process a few times, once again hold the treat in front of your dog, but do not say anything. Close your hand around the treat before your dog can take it. Do not pull your hand away, and be prepared for your dog to paw, lick, and even bark at your hand for the treat. After a few moments, once your dog settles down and waits patiently for a few seconds, open your hand and say "Take it" as your dog eats the treat. Repeat this exercise again and again until your dog waits for you to say "Take it."

The *leave it* cue is very similar to take it. However, wait until your dog fully understands the *take it* cue before you start teaching *leave it*. When you feel your pup has mastered *take it*, move on to *leave it*. Place a treat in the palm of your hand and hold it in front of your Shih Tzu. When he moves to take the treat, close your hand and say "Leave it." Repeat this step until he pulls away for a moment,

Practice *take it*, *leave it*, and *drop it* cues with a toy or other harmless object so that your dog has the training down pat by the time you really do need him to leave something alone.

waiting. Then, open your hand and say "Take it," allowing him to take the treat. Keep repeating this process until he understands the difference between the two cues. Over time, you will extend the pause between the *leave it* and *take it* cues, gradually building your Shih Tzu's patience. Eventually, he will be able to leave the treat until you give the cue to take it.

Once your Shih Tzu masters the *take it* and *leave it* cues with the treats in your hand, move your lessons to things on the ground that you don't want him to pick up. With your puppy on a loose leash, toss a treat behind and to the side of you, so that your puppy can see where it lands. Say "Leave it" as you toss the treat. If your Shih Tzu goes for the treat, use your body to gently block his way. Keep blocking him until he waits for your "Take it" cue. Repeat this lesson until he understands the treat-on-the-ground lesson in the same way as the treat-in-the-hand lesson.

There will be times when your Shih Tzu will see something on a walk or in the backyard that he wants to grab and chew on. To train your dog to leave something alone, place toys or food along your usual walking route. When your dog reaches for the item, give a short, quick tug on his leash and say "Leave it." Reward and praise him when he obeys. Repeat this lesson often—but be sure to let him take the object at times as well so that he doesn't feel slighted. Remember, keep all of your lessons positive!

The *take it*/*leave it* cues help your puppy understand that you are the leader, and that all good things (like food, treats, and hugs) come from you. It also helps your puppy avoid bad habits such as becoming possessive of his food or toys. You must always be in a position to take something away from your dog without him reacting aggressively. The *take it*/*leave it* cues, when taught correctly, are essential lessons that will benefit both you and your pup for life.

Likewise, the *drop it* cue is important because there will be times when your Shih Tzu will pick up something in his mouth that he shouldn't have. Whether that item is a poisonous plant or simply a living room pillow, your dog needs to be able to understand the importance and the immediacy of the *drop it* cue for his own safety (as well as the safety of your home!). Similar to *leave it*, when your dog picks up something he shouldn't, firmly say "Drop it" or "Leave it" and walk toward him to remove the item. Don't run toward him, or your dog will think you are starting a game of chase. Be sure to praise your dog when he drops the item.

SIT

This cue should be very easy to teach to your Shih Tzu because by this time your dog recognizes that he gets a treat when he obeys you. With the leash in your left hand, hold a small treat in your right, letting your dog smell or lick the treat but not take it. Move it away as you say "Sit," your hand rising slowly over the dog's head

Begin training indoors, then gradually move outside, where there are more distractions present. Be sure to keep your pup on a leash until you are sure he has learned obedience.

so that he looks upward. In doing so, he will bend his knees and sit. When this has been accomplished, give him the food reward and lavish him with praise.

If your Shih Tzu starts to back up when you raise the food treat over his head, try instead to teach the lesson with two hands. Place your second hand behind your dog's rear end and, when he backs up to see the food treat in your hand, he'll feel your other hand behind him and naturally go into a *sit* position. Practice the exercise this way a few times and soon the dog will understand that he is expected to sit. Always praise him with every successful exercise.

DOWN

When your dog is confident with the *sit* cue, you can introduce *down*. Gentle training is the key here, as dogs do not like to be forced into a submissive position. Depending on your Shih Tzu's temperament, you may or may not encounter difficulties with the *down* cue. If yours is a dominant "top-dog" male, you will have to approach the cue gingerly; for a mellow female, the cue shouldn't take more than a treat and a little sweet talk.

With your Shih Tzu sitting by your left leg, as with the *sit*, hold the leash in your left hand and a treat in your right. Place your left hand on top of the dog's shoulders (without pushing) and hold the treat under his nose, saying "Down" in a quiet tone of voice. Gradually move the treat along the floor, in front of the dog, all the while talking gently. He will follow the food, lowering himself down. When

The *down* cue can be difficult for some dogs to master, as the submissive posture goes against their nature. However, it's a helpful training tool in the long run.

Can Your Dog Pass the Canine Good Citizen® Test?

Once your Shih Tzu is ready for advanced training, you can start training him for the American Kennel Club Canine Good Citizen® program. This program is for dogs that are trained to behave at home, out in the neighborhood, and in the city. It's easy and fun to do. Once your dog learns basic obedience and good canine manners, a CGC evaluator gives your dog ten basic tests. If he passes, he's awarded a Canine Good Citizen® certificate. Many trainers offer classes with the test as the final "graduation" class. To find an evaluator in your area, go to www.akc.org/events/cgc/cgc_bystate.cfm.

Many therapy dogs and guide dogs are required to pass the Canine Good Citizen® test in order to help as working dogs in the community. There are ten specific tests that a dog must pass in order to pass the Canine Good Citizen® test. A well-trained dog will:

1. Let a friendly stranger approach and talk to his owner.
2. Let a friendly stranger pet him.
3. Be comfortable being groomed and examined by a friendly stranger.
4. Walk on a leash and show that he is in control and not overly excited.
5. Move through a crowd politely and confidently.
6. Sit and stay on command.
7. Come when called.
8. Behave calmly around another dog.
9. Not bark at or react to a surprise distraction.
10. Show that he can be left with a trusted person away from his owner.

In order to help your dog pass the AKC CGC test, first enroll him in a series of basic training classes and CGC training classes. You can find classes and trainers near you by searching the AKC website. When you feel that your Shih Tzu is ready to take the test, locate an AKC-approved CGC evaluator to set up a test date, or sign up for a test that is held at a local AKC dog show or training class. For more information about the AKC Canine Good Citizen® program, visit the website at www.akc.org/events.cgc.

his elbows touch the floor, you can release the treat and give praise, but try to get him to remain there for a few seconds before getting up. Gradually, the time of the *down* exercise can be increased.

Some Toy dogs don't respond to the *down* cue too readily—partially because they're already pretty close to the floor in the first place. You can try to teach the *down* cue with your Shih Tzu on your lap, facing forward. Use the food treat at the dog's nose and lower it below the level of your lap. The dog will squat down and assume the desired position. After you've practiced the cue a few times this way, you can place your puppy on the chair or couch next to you and try the cue there. Always praise your puppy for assuming the position. Once your Shih Tzu recognizes the cue, you can begin to work on the floor again.

STAY

The stay cue can be taught with your dog in either a *sit* or a *down* position, as usual with the leash in your left hand and the treat in your right. Allow him to lick the treat as you say "Stay," while standing directly in front of the dog, having moved from your position beside him. Silently count to about five, then move back to your original position alongside him, allowing your dog to have the treat while giving him lavish praise.

Keep practicing *stay* for a few days, then gradually increase the distance between you, using your hand with your palm facing the dog as an indication that he must stay. Soon you should be able to do this exercise without a leash in an enclosed area, and your Shih Tzu will stay for increasingly longer periods of time. Always give lots of praise upon completion of the exercise. Remember to have patience, building up duration and distance a little at a time.

STAND

There will be many occasions when you need your dog to stand still. Your veterinarian will appreciate your efforts if you have trained your Shih Tzu to stand still for his examination. Likewise, if you have a show dog, it's ideal if your dog can stand perfectly statuesque while the judge is reviewing him. In everyday life, you may want your Shih Tzu to stand by your side when coming to an intersection, especially on a rainy day when the usual *sit* position (part of the *heel* lesson) isn't particularly smart. During grooming sessions, the stand and down positions are also particularly useful.

Start with the puppy sitting by your side. Holding the leash in your left hand and a food treat in your right hand, place the food treat at the dog's nose so that he can see it. As you move your hand slowly forward, the dog will stand to be closer to the treat. As he does this, say "Stand." Give him the treat and praise him. Repeat this lesson until your Shih Tzu stands without the motivation of a treat.

WAIT

When you open the front door, have you ever turned to see your dog bolting through the entryway, and all you can do is yell and give chase? Don't you wish you could freeze that little furry body in place before he made it past the front porch? The *wait* cue will do just this.

Start teaching the *wait* cue in a doorway somewhere inside the house. Keeping your Shih Tzu behind you, slowly open the door so that you can walk through it. When your Shih Tzu tries to follow you through the doorway (or tries to get in front of you), block him with your body. Don't say anything just yet. When he pauses to let you through the doorway first, open the door a little more and say "Through" or "OK," and let him walk through the doorway. Do this a few times until he recognizes your positive cue. Then, when he hesitates to let you pass through the doorway first, say "Wait." Keep repeating these two cues until he understands that he must wait until you give him a cue to move through the doorway. Practice this lesson through different doorways around the house, finally moving to the back door, and then the front.

COME

This cue is another important lesson that your Shih Tzu must learn as a puppy. It could save your dog's life. Your Shih Tzu will love to come to you when called as long as you keep the call positive and fun. The idea is to invite him, using a happy "Come" cue to return, offering a treat and giving lots of praise when he does so. Never call him to come to you for a reprimand. You only want positive associations with your call, so that your dog is always excited to come back to you.

Start practicing the *come* cue in an enclosed yard. Keep your dog on a long leash at first. Walk a short distance from your Shih Tzu, and then get his attention by calling his name or clapping your hands. When the pup turns to look at you, call to him with a happy voice using his name, "Puppy, come!" He should come running toward you in expectation of a treat and lots of praise. If he doesn't

The *come* cue is perhaps the most useful of all, as it will help you wrangle your dog whenever he is off leash in everyday life.

Use small, nutritious treats or pieces of your dog's kibble as rewards for a job well done. Positive reinforcement is the suggested and preferred method of training advocated by most animal behaviorists nowadays.

come, give the leash a slight tug, pulling him toward you. Grasp his collar and give a treat. Holding his collar in your hand while you give him the treat is important, because he will start to associate your holding his collar with the treat. This will help you in the future, when you start to teach your Shih Tzu other behaviors using his collar.

Keep practicing the *come* cue at least ten or twelve times a day, until your puppy comes to you when called—not for treats, but simply for your verbal praise.

HEEL

A dog trained to heel will walk politely alongside his handler without pulling. The *heel* cue will also help you keep control of your Shih Tzu if he is uncomfortable around strangers. To teach it, hold the leash in your left hand while the dog assumes the *sit* position next to your left leg. Hold the end of the leash in your right hand, but also take hold of the leash lower down with your left hand. You will use your left hand to control the dog and hold him close to your side. Step forward with your left foot, saying the word "heel." To begin, take just three steps, allowing your Shih Tzu to walk at your side. Then, cue him to sit again. Repeat this procedure until he carries out the task without pulling. Once he masters three steps, you can increase the number of strides to five, seven, and so on. Give verbal praise at the end of each exercise. Once you are done, let him enjoy a free run to blow off some steam.

Many dogs respond to heel training automatically, while others can be quite stubborn. Don't let your Shih Tzu walk you! In time, your dog will realize that his master is one who knows the way, the speed, and the direction of his walk.

FIRST IN CLASS

When you first get a puppy or new dog, enroll in a young-dog training class such as puppy kindergarten or basic obedience. All of the basic cues are introduced in these classes by professional dog trainers. They will help you learn more about these training techniques and give you a basic foundation for training that you can build on throughout your Shih Tzu's life.

Read up on training techniques before working with your Shih Tzu, and concentrate on staying positive. Training a puppy requires time and commitment, but you will be glad you did it in the long run. The key is to practice, practice, practice. Keep in mind that your dog is never done training. If you don't keep up your dog's skills and practice with him daily, he will begin to forget his training and attempt to get his way. The reward for training a Shih Tzu lasts for your dog's whole lifetime in the form of a polite and obedient companion dog who adores you. What greater reward is there than that?

HIGHER LEARNING

Now that you've had your new Shih Tzu for a few months, socializing him with your family, friends, and neighbors and teaching him basic training cues such as sit and stay, you may want to know what you can do next.

The American Kennel Club is the perfect place to start your research. First, find the nearest American Kennel Club dog club in your area and discover what types of training courses are offered. Most clubs have basic obedience classes, including puppy kindergarten or the AKC S.T.A.R. Puppy Program. These classes will help provide a basic training foundation for your Shih Tzu and will benefit your pup throughout his life. Having trouble finding an AKC club near you? Search the AKC website's training clubs through its online directory at www.akc.org/events/obedience /training_clubs. The local club representative will be happy to help you find the right class or activity for you and your Shih Tzu.

Once you have completed basic training with your dog, there are many opportunities for advanced training. Consider activities like the Canine Good Citizen test or the Beginner Novice Obedience Class. An AKC club near you can help you learn more about these activities and also help you get involved with other Shih Tzu owners close by who are interested in keeping their dogs active and involved, just like you!

Take time to train your Shih Tzu, and you will deepen the bond with your pup. As your dog ages, it's important to continue training so that your relationship with your Shih Tzu can develop and grow stronger throughout his life.

At a Glance ...

Basic training is essential for all dogs in order to become well-behaved canine citizens.

. . . .

Getting and holding your dog's attention is the key to beginning any lesson. The easiest way to do this is with food treats and positive reinforcement.

. . . .

Sit, heel, down, stay, **and** ***come*** **are among the basic cues. These first lessons will help keep your dog safe and out of trouble. They will also help strengthen the bond between you and your Shih Tzu.**

. . . .

What's next, you ask? Research the American Kennel Club website for more information about all of the sports and activities you and your Shih Tzu can get involved with.

Food for Thought

In general, Shih Tzu are good eaters, though, as with all breeds, there can be the occasional finicky pup who will need that extra bit of encouragement. Most Shih Tzu owners consider their dogs their "babies" and naturally want to spoil them, but it's never a good idea to pander to your Shih Tzu's every whim. He'll never complain, but you may end up with a fussy, chubby child who insists upon fresh wild-caught salmon and filet mignon, medium rare—and nothing else!

SO MANY CHOICES

Today there is an enormous range of specially prepared foods available for dogs, many of which are scientifically balanced and formulated for particular age ranges and sizes. Which food you decide to buy is really a matter of personal preference, though your decision will undoubtedly be influenced by the type of food that was fed to your puppy by his breeder. Of course, you can make changes to his diet, but don't change suddenly from one food to another, or your Shih Tzu will likely get an upset stomach. Introduce new food gradually, over the course of a few weeks, until the old brand is phased out. There is usually no concern if you are only changing the flavor of food, while staying with the same brand. This can add some variety to the diet, which your Shih Tzu will appreciate. You can also add a little flavored stock to the food to tempt your canine's palate.

If you decide to feed your dog a dry product, make sure that you read the feeding instructions thoroughly. Some of these products need to be moistened, especially for youngsters. Dry food should also be stored carefully, preferably in airtight containers. There are two reasons for this: to keep the food fresher and to prevent unwanted guests (such as ants and mice) from inviting themselves to dinner. Bear in mind that the vitamin value of dry food declines if it not used fairly quickly, usually within about three months.

WET AND DRY

Should you take the dry road or the wet road to get to the land of good nutrition? The answer depends on what your particular dog needs (or doesn't need). Dry food has less fat than canned food, can help remove the plaque and tartar that builds up on a dog's teeth, gives dogs that satisfying crunchiness when they chew it, and costs less than wet food.

Dry food varieties are also the most calorie- and nutrient-dense, so you need less of it to provide the same amount of nutrition. It's also the most price-friendly. On the negative side, dry food has more preservatives and offers fewer flavors. Dry food is higher in carbohydrates, and the lesser brands often list soybean, corn, and other bulky starches as the main ingredients.

Wet foods, by contrast, offer an extensive array of appealing flavors, so you should have no trouble finding ones your dog will enjoy, but be prepared to pay more. Because wet food has a much higher fat content than dry, you'll need to offer your dog the correct amount so he doesn't gain unnecessary

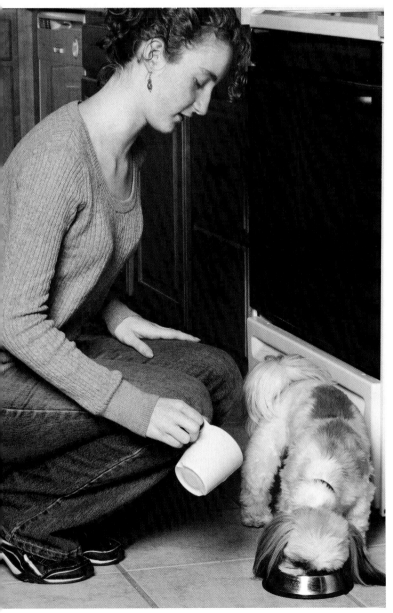

Research, talk to your breeder, and get advice from your vet when deciding what type of food to give your Shih Tzu. It's his fuel for life.

weight. That can happen more quickly than you think. Wet food is also higher in protein, which is good for a growing dog.

You don't have to worry about adding water to canned food, of course, but you will probably want to add a little water or broth to your dog's dry kibble. Many owners jazz up their dry food choice occasionally by mixing in a bit of wet food. Your Shih Tzu will love it.

There are also semimoist, raw, and frozen foods available. These foods are more expensive than wet or dry varieties. Talk to your veterinarian to learn more about these diets and decide if one is beneficial for your dog. You should also consult your veterinarian for advice on which foods are best for your Shih Tzu puppy and which are best as he matures into an adult.

NECESSARY NUTRIENTS

Dogs (like humans) need a combination of proteins, carbohydrates, fats, vitamins, and minerals in their diets to stay healthy. The percentage of each will change as your dog ages. And don't forget water! Here's a brief rundown of these necessary nutrients:

- **Proteins** are used for growth and the repairing of muscles, bones, and other body tissues. They also help produce antibodies, enzymes, and hormones.
- **Carbohydrates** are metabolized by the body into glucose, which is the body's main energy source.
- **Fats** provide the body with energy when no glucose is available. They are also important for proper function of the nervous system, the production of hormones, and vitamin support.
- **Vitamins** and **minerals** participate in the body's muscle and nerve functions, as well as assist in growing bone, promoting healing, maintaining a good metabolism, and balancing fluids.
- **Water** is essential for life, hydrating the body and flushing away toxins and waste. All dogs, big and small, require plenty of fresh drinking water to keep their bodies functioning at optimal performance and to avoid dehydration during extreme heat or exercise. Give your dog ample access to fresh water throughout the day. Change the water often.

COMPLETE AND BALANCED

Your Shih Tzu will only thrive if you feed him a complete and balanced diet, so look for food formulas labeled as such. The Association of American Feed Control Officials (AAFCO) has standardized the requirements for appropriate canine food

No Table Scraps!

As a general rule, do not feed your Shih Tzu people food, especially spicy, prepared foods. A lot of what we eat is dangerous for a dog to eat. While it's perfectly okay to add cooked carrots, chicken, or brown rice to your dog's dinner bowl, foods such as chocolate, onions, grapes, and nuts will make your Shih Tzu very ill.

A PIECE OF HISTORY

In ancient China, only royalty kept Shih Tzu, which were bred in the Forbidden City (the Chinese Imperial Palace in Beijing). The high regard the Chinese had for the Shih Tzu is reflected in the many pieces of art bearing the breed's likeness that have survived to this day.

Changing Diets

When you bring home your new Shih Tzu, be careful about changing to a completely different dog food right away. That quick change could make your dog sick. If you plan to switch from the food fed by his breeder, take home a small supply of the breeder's food to mix with your own. Make the change slowly to aid your puppy's adjustment to his new food.

formulas. Only foods that have been approved by the AAFCO are allowed to be labeled as "complete and balanced," meaning that they meet the nutritional standards for dogs at their various stages of life. Manufacturers earn this label either by conducting strictly controlled feeding trials or by matching their products to a detailed nutrient profile.

A complete and balanced diet consists of the proper proportion of vitamins, minerals, fats, protein, and carbohydrates necessary to promote your dog's growth and good health. Your dog's size and activity level will determine the amount of food he needs each day. Start by giving your Shih Tzu the amount of food that is suggested on the food's label, but keep an eye on him while he eats. The portion suggested may be larger than necessary. If you notice your Shih Tzu's waistline expanding or if his ribs feel more prominent, you'll need to adjust the portion accordingly. If you're unsure how much you should feed your little dog, ask your veterinarian for advice.

Like other Toy breeds, Shih Tzu that are younger than four months are more susceptible than bigger breeds to develop hypoglycemia (low blood sugar). One trigger is going too long without eating. Because of their small stomachs, puppies need to eat more frequently than adults. So be sure to feed him nutritionally balanced meals four or five times a day. Consult your veterinarian before adding vitamins, minerals, or any other supplements to your dog's regular food. Extra nutrients that are helpful for a larger dog's system can overwhelm a small dog's system. A Shih Tzu receiving a complete and balanced diet shouldn't need any supplements.

LIFESTAGE FOODS

Lifestage formulas have grown in popularity in recent years. You'll find many types marketed on store shelves, such as growth and reproduction formula (for puppies and pregnant/lactating females) and maintenance formula (for adult dogs). Ask your veterinarian's advice before starting your Shih Tzu on any specialty food varieties beyond these.

• **Puppy diets:** Growth formulas provide higher levels of fat, protein, and vitamins to sustain a young dog's normal growth rate. According to the AAFCO, the formula must contain at least 22 percent protein.

• **Adult diets:** AAFCO-approved adult maintenance diets must have at least 18 percent protein and 5 percent fat. Talk to your veterinarian before deciding what type of food is right for your dog.

• **Pregnant/lactating diets:** The same growth formulas you give puppies are recommended for pregnant/lactating females; these formulas are high in fat, protein, and vitamins.

• **Senior diets:** Older, less active dogs need fewer calories. The protein and fat content in these formulas can vary.

NUTRITIONAL NEEDS

Because of the enormous range of products available, you may find it difficult to decide which to choose without advice from your veterinarian, breeder, or an experienced Shih Tzu owner. Keep in mind that, in adulthood, an active dog will

require higher protein content than one that lives a more sedentary life. Regardless, though, the protein required by this small breed is never particularly high.

It is also worth mentioning that some Tibetan and Asian breeds are intolerant of dairy products. This can often be displayed as a rash or irritant patch on the tummy. Should this happen, eliminate milk, cheese, and eggs (check the dog-food labels for these ingredients) to see if this resolves the problem.

How many times a day you feed your adult Shih Tzu is mainly a matter of preference. Many people divide the daily portion into morning and evening meals; others prefer to give just one meal, perhaps with a light snack at the other end of the day. Most owners of Toy dogs feed them twice daily. Obviously, puppies need to be fed more frequently, but your dog's breeder will advise you in this regard. The transition to the adult feeding schedule should happen gradually.

As a dog gets older, his metabolism changes, so feeding requirements may also change, typically from his regular schedule to smaller meals perhaps three or four times a day. By then, you will know your dog well and should be able to adjust feeding accordingly. If you have any queries, your vet will certainly be able to guide you in the right direction.

Be sure to provide your pup with enough food and water when left in his crate throughout the day. But remember, that also means more potty breaks!

Free-Feeding Frenzy

If you leave a bowl of food out for your Shih Tzu all the time (which is called free-feeding), you could turn him into a picky eater—a bite here, a nibble there. He could turn his pug nose up at the food you offer, demanding something else. Dogs that are free-feeders are also more likely to become possessive of their food bowls. If you come near your dog's food bowl, he could begin growling at you, which is a dog's way of saying "Back off!" Dogs should never growl at their owners, as it could lead to other more serious behavioral problems of aggression.

TREATS

You don't want to appear heartless by denying your Shih Tzu treats of any kind. Treats are fine, as long as they are nutritious and you only provide them occasionally. Pet stores offer a range of snack foods for your dog, but as with regular food, you need to check the ingredients on the packages. Crunchy (dry) treats are usually best for your dog's teeth and waistline.

You can also give your Shih Tzu a few homemade treats, such as veggies and fruits, and even cheese and meats. But you must be selective. Dogs can't tolerate all produce, and they shouldn't be fed any foods that are high in sugar or fat.

Here are a few suggestions for treats from home: broccoli stems, carrots, green beans, and peas; apples, bananas, and pears; reduced-fat cheeses; and cooked, lean meat. Feed your dog small portions only; otherwise you can seriously upset his system.

Warning: There are certain foods that are very dangerous for dogs, causing reactions that range from vomiting and diarrhea to death. To find out more about what foods to keep away from your dog, go to www.dogchannel.com and search for "people food."

THE BOTTOM LINE

What and how much you choose to feed your Shih Tzu are major factors in his overall health and how long he lives. The longest-lived of all dogs, Toy breeds are still susceptible to health problems if they do not have a well-balanced diet with appropriate portions. Keep treats to a minimum: a couple of extra pounds on a big dog may not be a matter of concern, but on a small Shih Tzu they can seriously compromise his health. Research the nutritional content of anything you plan to buy before you go shopping. At the store, don't let fancy packaging distract you from reading and carefully considering the ingredients in a bag or can of dog food. If you have any questions about your dog's nutrition, consult your veterinarian. Always bear in mind that your Shih Tzu's well-being and health is in your hands.

At a Glance ...

Your Shih Tzu's good-quality diet will be appropriate to his age, breed size, and individual activity level. Your veterinarian can help you determine your dog's dietary needs.

· ·

Your breeder will be a good source of advice about how best to feed your puppy and how to change the type of food, amounts, and feeding schedule as the puppy grows up.

· ·

Avoid table scraps, as they can add weight or upset your dog's digestion. Shih Tzu are known to have trouble with dairy products; furthermore, some people foods can actually be toxic to dogs.

· ·

If you choose to feed your dog a diet other than a complete traditional dog food, only attempt to do so after consulting your veterinarian.

CHAPTER NINE

Groomed to Perfection

The minute you bring home a Shih Tzu, you enter the ranks of dog groomers (albeit the amateur, nonpaid division) because while this Toy dog is short in stature, he's certainly long in coat—easily the breed's most recognizable feature. In his natural, unshorn state, the Shih Tzu sports a full-length, floor-sweeping coat. Whether you choose to keep your dog's coat long (as it must be for showing) or cut it, you will be doing a whole lot of grooming.

Most owners of pet-quality Shih Tzu prefer to keep their dogs' coats short in a pet clip (also known as a puppy cut). If you choose this option, you will probably want to use the services of a professional groomer. A pet trim will require visits to the groomer every six to eight weeks and will need careful grooming attention at home in between visits.

COAT CARE

All dogs should be introduced to regular grooming at a very early age, but this is especially true for the Shih Tzu. Within three or four days of your new puppy's arrival, set aside a few minutes a day for grooming sessions. You can begin by teaching your dog to stand on a sturdy table and accept gentle grooming with a soft brush. Consider purchasing a grooming table to make these sessions easier for you and your pet. This special table is equipped with a nonskid pad, an adjustable height lever, and a noose and an arm (for holding the dog in place), all of which make grooming easier on your dog and your back. When the dog is used to standing on the table, teach him to lie on his side; it is much easier to groom a fully coated Shih Tzu this way. With your dog in this position, you can reach all the awkward places more easily.

Grooming sessions will lengthen as your dog matures and his coat grows out. The Shih Tzu usually grows an adult coat between ten to twelve months of age. During this transition, your dog's coat will mat more quickly and frequently than it did before. Once he's through this transition stage, however, this won't happen as much. But you will still need to be diligent about brushing. The Shih Tzu has a double coat, and it is the inner, cottony one that usually becomes matted.

Your Shih Tzu's easily tangled coat will need brushing after every outdoor play session.

To brush your dog, begin by placing him on his back on the grooming table and misting his coat with a spray bottle containing a solution of water and canine conditioner. Now brush his exposed underside with a pin brush or a slicker brush.

Move your Shih Tzu into a standing position, and brush his sides, back, and legs. Always brush his back toward his tail and his sides toward the ground. Finally, carefully brush his head. Then run a metal comb through the entire coat to make sure all the mats are untangled. Although you will remove a certain amount of dead hair as you groom, do not take out too much at any one time (except while he's shedding).

CHECK KEY AREAS

Trim away your Shih Tzu's hair in certain places to make the dog more comfortable. You can carefully cut away a little hair just inside the armpits to prevent knots from forming there.

The back end of the Shih Tzu and his feet will always need to be checked regularly, and the underside of the pads should be carefully trimmed to prevent painful knots from forming between them. Another area that will need special attention is the coat growth just behind the ears because this hair is usually finer and more prone to knotting.

THE TOPKNOT

What's that dapper topknot you see so many Shih Tzu sporting? Is it just an excuse for these Toy dogs to prance about in a stylish bow? The bow may be all about style, but the topknot itself serves an actual purpose: it keeps a Shih Tzu's face and head hair away from his eyes, nose, and mouth. That means better access to the face for cleaning and less irritation for the dog. By around five months of age, your Shih Tzu will have sufficient head furnishings to form a topknot.

To create a topknot, you will need a metal comb and several tiny elastic bands. You can buy special little bands at pet-supply stores and dog shows or purchase dental elastics through an orthodontist. Here are a couple types of topknots and how to create them. (*Warning:* always be careful when working around your dog's eyes).

Puppy Topknot

1. With a comb, carefully part the hair between the eyes, from the inner corner of one eye to the inner corner of the other.

Keep the Face Clean

In between baths, owners will need to tidy up the Shih Tzu's face. Corn starch or baby powder is handy to whiten and dry the face and moustache. A self-rinse shampoo can be applied to a soiled area on the face with a cotton ball and then wiped off with a clean, soft towel. If you find that your Shih Tzu has an unusually wet and smelly face, you may want to apply the self-rinse shampoo daily to keep him looking and smelling good.

2. Gather and section the hair into an inverted V.

3. Secure the hair with an elastic band.

Casual Topknot

1. With a comb, carefully part the hair between the eyes, from the inner corner of one eye to the inner corner of the other.

2. Lift the hair you're holding forward and make a part across the middle of the skull.

3. Brush the first section of hair forward.

4. Tie an elastic band around this section.

5. To create another section, run the comb through the hair toward the back of one ear, across the head, to the back of the other ear.

6. Gather this section together and band it.

7. For that extra bit of style, tie a bow on the first section, then join the two sections with another band.

Another important final touch, common to all Shih Tzu, is the part that runs from the back of the head to the tail. Many Shih Tzu have the unfortunate habit of shaking after their grooming sessions are complete, but a carefully made part will help the hair fall back into place.

EYES AND EARS

Hair grows inside your Shih Tzu's ears, so it is necessary to remove it carefully, either with blunt-ended tweezers or with your fingertips. If you remove just a few hairs at a time, it should be painless.

Every dog's ears must be kept clean as well. To do this, use a cotton ball and a special ear cleanser, usually a liquid or powder that you can get at a pet store. Always take extreme care not to delve into the ear canal or you could damage it. For that reason, it's better not to use a cotton swab unless you have a well-trained hand and an even better-trained dog.

If your dog has been shaking his head or scratching at his ears, he may have an infection or ear mites. A thick brown discharge and bad smell are indicative of these problems, so veterinary consultation is needed right away.

You must also keep your Shih Tzu's eyes clean. If a coat is not groomed thoroughly around the eyes, they can develop a buildup of mucus. Such buildup is not only uncomfortable for your Shih Tzu but also can scratch his eyes. Tear stains, which are common in many breeds, should be cleaned away as well. To clean around the eyes, use eye wipes or cleaning pads made for dogs. Some people also recommend patting a bit of cornstarch on the area under each eye to keep it dry.

At any sign of eye injury or if the eye turns blue, take your dog to the veterinarian immediately. If an eye injury is dealt with quickly, it can often be repaired; if neglected, it can lead to loss of sight.

BATHING BASICS

Show dogs are usually bathed before each show, but a pet Shih Tzu can be bathed less frequently. Purchase a quality dog shampoo; do not use a human product because it is too harsh for the dog's coat and will dry it out. When bathing, be

When you bathe your Shih Tzu, use canine-specific shampoo and spray-on conditioner. And take extra care to avoid getting soap or water in his eyes.

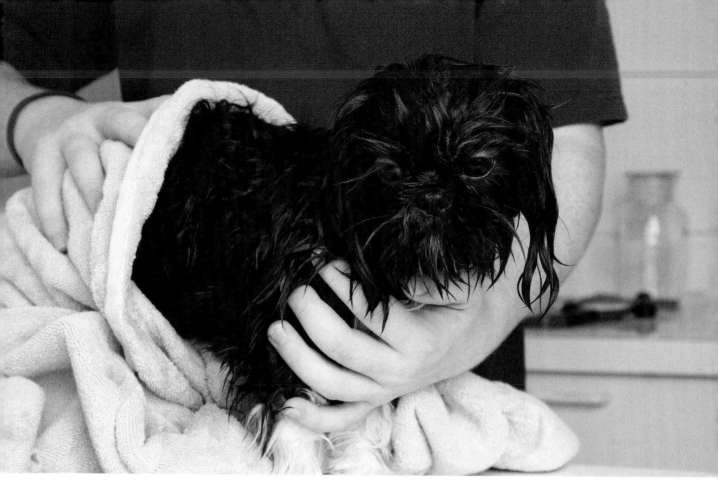

After bathing, pat your Shih Tzu's coat dry to avoid creating painful knots.

sure to test the temperature of the water on the back of your own hand before it touches your dog. It should be warm, not extremely hot or cold. After wetting your Shih Tzu's coat, stroke in the shampoo gently. Do not rub, as this will create knots. The shampoo must be rinsed out thoroughly before applying a conditioner, which should also be completely rinsed away. Use a towel to pat—not rub—your dog's coat dry to avoid creating painful knots.

When drying, it is important to groom the coat thoroughly as you do so, much as you would during a routine grooming session. If you just leave the coat to dry naturally, or blow-dry without brushing, you will have a very unkempt-looking Shih Tzu on your hands! When grooming without bathing, it is important to use a conditioning spray or at least water spray because the ends will break if you groom when the coat is completely dry. Antitangle or conditioning spray should be applied generously to any mats. Leave the spray in for a few minutes, then tease out the mat carefully, using your fingers or a wide-toothed comb. Always tease the mat from the inside outward; otherwise, it will simply get tighter.

NAIL CARE

Nails must always be kept trimmed, but how frequently they need clipping depends on the surface upon which your Shih Tzu walks. Dogs that live primarily on carpets or on grass will need more frequent attention to their nails than those who regularly exercise on a hard surface.

Your Shih Tzu must be trained to accept nail clipping from an early age because long nails can get caught in the coat. Take great care not to cut the quick, which is the blood vessel that runs through the nail, because this is painful for the dog. In light-colored nails, the quick can usually be seen and avoided. The quick in dark-colored nails is difficult if not impossible to see, and you're more likely to accidently cut one. Cutting just a sliver of nail at a time is the safest approach. In any case, it is a good idea to keep a styptic pencil or some styptic powder on hand to staunch any bleeding.

If you hear the click, click, click of your pup's nails on the ground, it's time to get out the clippers.

ORAL HYGIENE

A Shih Tzu needs to have his teeth brushed regularly, not only to maintain friendships but to also prevent medical problems. Plaque and tartar buildup can lead to gum disease, which can be the start of more serious diseases of the internal organs, such as the heart.

As with bathing, you should introduce tooth brushing while your Shih Tzu is still a puppy. Start by rubbing your finger around his gums and over his puppy teeth. Make it a good experience for him by praising him and petting him a lot throughout the process. When your dog seems ready and used to the sensation, you can start the real brushing.

It's not as easy to brush a Shih Tzu's pearly whites as it is to brush those of a big dog because the Shih Tzu's teeth and mouth are small. Use a small doggie toothbrush or a child-size human toothbrush. If you have problems with the toothbrush, try premoistened dental wipes with plaque inhibitors. You can gently wipe over tooth surfaces and along the gumline.

You'll need to hold your dog's head still with one hand, while you brush with the other. If possible, brush each tooth in a circular motion, with the brush held at an angle to the gumline, and scrub the tops, fronts, and sides of each tooth. Be sure to use canine toothpaste, with doggie-delicious flavors such as chicken or beef; human toothpaste will make dogs sick.

While brushing, look for signs of plaque, tartar, and gum disease. Redness, swelling, bad breath, receding gums, and discolored enamel along the gumline are all red flags. If you notice any of these signs, schedule an appointment with your veterinarian. As a good rule of thumb, most vets suggest you take your dog for yearly dental checkups and professional teeth cleaning regardless of his oral health condition.

THE DIRTY WORK

If you see your dog scooting his behind across the floor or licking his rectum, it probably means that his anal glands are full and need to be expressed (evacuated). A dog's anal glands are located on either side of the anal opening. Sometimes they become blocked and require evacuation. Experienced breeders often express the anal glands themselves, but pet owners would be well advised to leave this to vets or professional groomers. An inexperienced owner can damage the glands. In any case, this is one messy, smelly job that most people prefer to avoid.

Good Teeth = Good Health

Home dental care is vital to your Shih Tzu's health. Studies prove that good oral hygiene (taking care of your dog's teeth by regular brushing and a checkup by the vet) can add three to five years to a dog's life. In other words, brushing your Shih Tzu's teeth means you'll have him around for a lot longer!

Grooming Shopping List

Here are the items you need to groom your Shih Tzu:

BATHING

☐ A handheld spray attachment for your tub or sink

☐ A rubber mat for the dog to stand on

☐ A tearless dog shampoo and crème-rinse conditioner
(don't use human products)

☐ Towels (a chamois is best)

☐ A pet hair dryer (you can use your own, but set it on low heat)

☐ Spritz-on dry shampoos (handy in case you need a quick clean-up
to get rid of dirt or odor)

BRUSHING COAT

☐ Soft pin brush or slicker brush

☐ Metal comb

BRUSHING TEETH

☐ Dog toothbrush or child's toothbrush

☐ Dog toothpaste (don't use human toothpaste)

☐ Premoistened canine dental wipes

CLEANING EARS

☐ Cotton balls or wipes

☐ Liquid ear-cleaning solution

DESIGNING THE TOPKNOT

☐ Metal comb

☐ Spray bottle

☐ Small elastic hair bands

☐ Bow (optional)

TRIMMING NAILS

☐ Dog nail cutters (scissor- or guillotine-type) or a grinder

☐ Nail file (to file down jagged edges)

☐ Styptic powder (in case you cut the quick)

WIPING EYES

☐ Doggie eye wipes or hydrogen peroxide

☐ Cotton balls

☐ Cornstarch

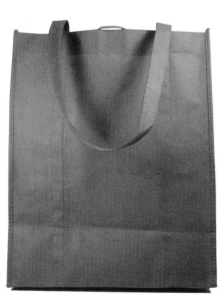

CALLING ALL GROOMERS

Because of the high level of grooming maintenance required by a Shih Tzu, many owners opt to hire a groomer to do the more difficult tasks described above. To find a good groomer, ask your veterinarian, breeder, or other friends who own coated dogs for recommendations. Tell them you're looking specifically for a groomer who knows how to correctly groom a Shih Tzu. If you plan on showing your dog, you can learn a lot about show grooming by talking to other exhibitors at the shows. Your breeder can likely assist you with show grooming and recommend a mentor to get you started.

Do not hesitate to ask the groomer lots of questions about the services the shop provides. Make sure your dog's experience there will be as painless and comfortable as possible. How are difficult dogs handled? What kind of shampoo is used? What method is used for drying the dogs? Where will your dog be kept while waiting to be groomed or picked up by you? The more you ask, the quicker you will be able to assess whether you've found the right groomer for your Shih Tzu.

Ear Check

Sometimes when dogs play outdoors, they get stuff in their ears, such as seeds, burrs, and foxtails—anything that tends to stick to fur. Check your Shih Tzu's ears for these things when he comes in from playing outdoors. If left in the ear, they will cause your dog pain and possibly damage his hearing. If you find something and cannot safely remove it at home, take your dog to the vet right away.

At a Glance ...

As a Shih Tzu owner, you must be prepared from the outset to make grooming a big part of your life.

Whether you keep your dog in full coat or a pet trim is your choice, but both coats require attention.

Using a grooming table, teach your dog to lie on his side for grooming to enable you to get all of the hard-to-reach places.

How frequently you bathe your dog will depend on whether yours is a show dog and on how often the coat gets dirty.

A Shih Tzu owner must know how to avoid matting, how to detangle a mat if it occurs, and how to put up a topknot.

Care of the ears, eyes, nails, and anal glands should be part of your weekly grooming routine.

CHAPTER TEN

Healthy and Happy

Routine daily care is important to keep your Shih Tzu healthy. The most important responsibility of all pet owners is to ensure the long life and good health of their dogs. Don't wait until your Shih Tzu is already having a problem to take him to the vet.

The best way to ensure your dog's good health is to maintain a consistent wellness program. Make sure he eats the right food, gets regular exercise, stays well-groomed, and visits

Take your pup to the vet within the first few days of bringing him home. After he's completed all of his puppy shots, he'll need routine health checkups annually.

the veterinarian routinely. Regular health checks will help catch and treat any serious illnesses early.

VISIT THE VET

A knowledgeable, trustworthy vet is the most important partner in keeping your Shih Tzu healthy. As part of your puppy preparation, find a veterinarian before you get a Shih Tzu. Start looking for a good veterinarian about a month or two before you bring home a new Shih Tzu puppy. It will give you time to meet several potential veterinarians, observe the conditions of the clinic, and meet the staff to determine whether it's a good fit for you. It's definitely best to find a good veterinarian when you don't actually need one—rather than scrambling to find one in the midst of a medical crisis.

If you do not already have a vet for other family pets, select carefully. Ask for recommendations from your breeder or friends who have dogs and whose opinions you trust. Location is always an important factor: after all, you must be able to get your dog to the vet quickly in an emergency, and the vet must be able

A PIECE OF HISTORY

The "chrysanthemum-faced" Shih Tzu is full of life. The breed's facial hair growth earned it this flowery nickname. Early Chinese writings dating back as far as 1400 BC highly valued the flower as a medical herb believed to possess the power of life. One Chinese sage wrote, "If you would be happy for a lifetime, grow chrysanthemums." Likewise, if you would be happy for a lifetime, get a Shih Tzu.

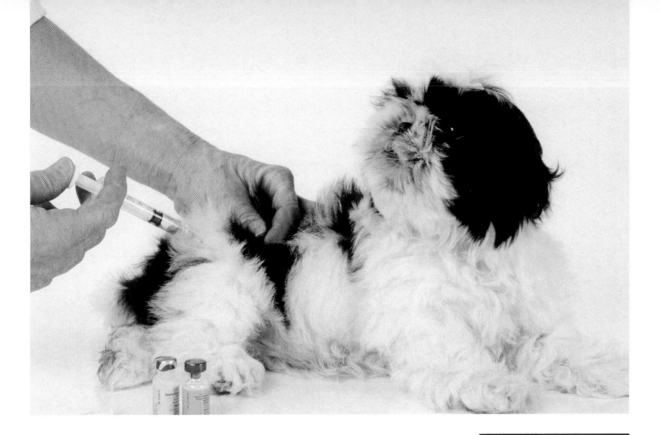

to respond rapidly when needed. If you live in a rural area, choose a vet who has plenty of experience dealing with small animals and is practiced in the special needs of Toy dogs. Many rural veterinarians have a great deal of experience with farm animals but limited experience with dogs.

Because the Shih Tzu has an amiable personality, your dog will probably enjoy visits to the vet, at least for routine examinations. Contact your vet before you take your pup in for his first visit—preferably on the way home from the breeder; it will give you and your puppy a chance to build rapport for future visits. Your new puppy can see the vet's office and meet everyone in a calm, welcoming environment. He won't be anxious when he comes back a few days later for a health exam and vaccinations.

EXAMS AND VACCINATIONS

If you purchased your puppy from a dedicated breeder, all necessary care will have been provided for the dam (mother), as well as her litter. Your pup's mother will have had regular health check-ups, boosters, and a worming routine. All of these health measures, combined with the natural immunities passed on through the dam, will help provide your puppy with greater immunity than would otherwise be the case. This natural disease resistance usually lasts from about eight to ten weeks of age, which is why it's important to take your pup to a vet as soon as possible to bolster his immune system for later in life.

Your puppy's first exam will consist of an overall assessment to ensure he doesn't have any problems that you aren't already aware of. At this time, the vet will also set up a schedule for your puppy's vaccinations, based on the information your breeder gave you about the pup's unfinished vaccination needs. Your Shih Tzu puppy should have had his first set of shots before he left his breeder. Routine vaccinations vary slightly, depending on the area in which you live and

Vac to Basics

The American Veterinary Medical Association (AVMA) recommends certain CORE vaccines for your puppy. These vaccines protect your Shih Tzu from diseases that are very dangerous to your puppy, such as canine hepatitis and rabies. Many of these CORE vaccines are mandatory in certain states. The rabies vaccine, for example, is required in all fifty states. Your vet will tell you which vaccinations your puppy needs. You can read more about vaccines on the AVMA website, www.avma.org.

the particular risks that your puppy will face. Many veterinarians have different opinions about which vaccines are best for your puppy, but most recommend about three different shots given every three to four weeks after you bring in your puppy for his first checkup.

Your vet will advise you when boosters are due and when your dog can go to public places after the vaccination course is complete. Many vets now send reminder notices for boosters, but you should still make a note on your calendar. If overdue, it may be necessary to give the full vaccination program again.

Some people prefer not to subject their animals to routine vaccinations and opt instead for a homeopathic alternative. If you prefer to go this route, you will need to follow a practicing homeopathic veterinarian's instructions to the letter. Also bear in mind that many towns require dogs to be vaccinated for rabies in order to receive a dog license; likewise, it will be difficult to find a boarding kennel or doggy day care that accepts a dog without proof of a rabies vaccination.

RECOGNIZING SIGNS OF ILL HEALTH

The more you know about your dog, the better prepared you will be to raise a healthy Shih Tzu. Keep a notebook or dog diary on your pet's behavior and record all health information, especially after every veterinary visit. It will help keep track of any disconcerting new behaviors or bring attention to any odd health or behavioral patterns.

While spending time with your Shih Tzu and especially while grooming him, take note of his demeanor and watch for any bumps or physical anomalies. Keep an eye out for anything amiss: an ill Shih Tzu may stop eating his food or seem dull and listless, possibly carrying his tail down. His eyes, usually bright

CORE Vaccines
Check with your vet, but all puppies should receive vaccines for the following diseases.

CONDITION	TREATMENT	PROGNOSIS	VACCINE NEEDED
ADENOVIRUS-2 (immunizes against Adenovirus-1, the agent of infectious canine hepatitis)	No curative therapy for infectious hepatitis; treatment geared toward minimizing neurologic effects, shock, hemorrhage, secondary infections	Self-limiting but cross-protects against infectious hepatitis, which is highly contagious and can be mild to rapidly fatal	Recommended
DISTEMPER	No specific treatment; supportive treatment (IV fluids, antibiotics)	High mortality rates	Highly recommended
PARVOVIRUS-2	No specific treatment; supportive treatment (IV fluids, antibiotics)	Highly contagious to young puppies; high mortality rates	Highly recommended
RABIES	No treatment	Fatal	Required

and alive, may seem to lose their sparkle, and his coat may look dull. Changes in toileting habits may also be an indication if ill health. Diarrhea usually clears up within twenty-four hours, but if it continues for longer than this, especially if you see blood, you will need to visit your vet. The same is true for vomiting.

Increased thirst and frequency of urination can also indicate a problem. Contact your vet if you notice your Shih Tzu emptying his entire water bowl in one sitting. This could indicate diabetes or a bladder infection.

GROOMING CONSIDERATIONS

Always bring your Shih Tzu to the vet's office well groomed with his coat in clean condition as a courtesy to the staff. A matted Shih Tzu is an embarrassment for everyone involved (not least of all, your poor dog) and can make for a difficult exam. Don't worry about grooming in an emergency situation, however; your vet will fully understand, and time may be of utmost importance.

DENTAL CARE

Keeping teeth in good condition is your responsibility, and you owe this to your Shih Tzu. Regular dental care promotes healthy teeth, fresh breath, a healthy heart, and a longer life. Dental problems do not just stop inside the mouth. When gums are infected, all sorts of health problems can subsequently arise, spreading through the system and sometimes even resulting in death. Because of the small size of their mouths, Toy dogs are more prone to dental problems than larger dogs. Crowding and missing teeth are the most common dental problems in Toy dogs.

The veterinarian should give your Shih Tzu a thorough dental evaluation at six months of age to assess whether all of your pup's permanent teeth have

It's your job to check your Shih Tzu for any changes in his appearance or behavior between his annual visits to the vet.

Things to watch for:
- ☐ Has your Shih Tzu gained a few too many pounds or suddenly lost weight?
- ☐ Are his teeth clean and white?
- ☐ Is he going to the bathroom more frequently, drinking more water than usual?
- ☐ Does he have a hard time going to the bathroom?
- ☐ Are there any changes in his appetite?
- ☐ Does he appear short of breath, lazy, or overly tired?
- ☐ Does he limp or have a hard time walking around?

These can be signs of serious health problems that you should discuss with your vet as soon as they appear. It's especially important for older dogs because even small changes can be a sign of something serious.

Routine oral care can help avoid periodontal disease, which leads to other serious health risks.

grown in properly. Team up with the vet for the best possible dental care regimen, consisting of both yearly veterinary checkups and ongoing at-home care. A home-care schedule should combine weekly tooth brushing and occasional crunchy treats to help scrape away tartar and plaque. Safe chew toys and treats, like carrots for example, are great dental aids. However, with the Shih Tzu, take care that certain chews do not leave sticky debris in this breed's long coat. (See chapter 9, "Grooming to Perfection", for details on brushing your dog's teeth.)

CHECKING FOR PARASITES

It is essential to keep your dog's coat in top-notch condition; even a modest parasite infestation can transmit diseases and cause your dog's skin and coat health to deteriorate. It is difficult to see parasites, especially under the Shih Tzu's heavy coat, but if you catch sight of even one flea, you can be sure that more are lurking under the surface. Your daily grooming sessions are an excellent opportunity to check for any unwanted critters. There are many good preventive aids available for external parasites and pests, including the most prevalent—fleas, ticks, and mites. Your vet will advise you about which remedies work best.

Fleas: Fleas aren't just itchy and annoying for your dog; they can also cause disease. Chances are your Shih Tzu is going to get fleas at some point. Luckily, there are many ways to fight fleas; the infestation may be difficult to prevent, but it's relatively simple to treat. You'll need to treat both your dog and your home to completely eradicate these pests. First kill the adult fleas, then control the development of pre-adult fleas; your veterinarian can advise you on a variety of over-the-counter or prescription remedies, from squeeze-on topical liquid treatments to ingestible pill medication. Treat your home at the same time with an insect growth regulator spray and an insecticide to kill the adult fleas. Be sure to treat all carpets, furniture, bedding, hidden crevices around the house, and other areas where your Shih Tzu likes to hang out.

Ticks: Ticks are problematic for outdoor dogs because they can transmit nasty diseases such as Lyme disease (borreliosis), which can also spread to humans. Discuss the threat of ticks with your veterinarian; if you live in a tick-prone area, he may have a suggested course of preventive action.

Mites: Regularly check your dog for ear mites. They cannot be seen, but a brown discharge with some odor from the ear is a clear indication that they are present. A suitable ear treatment will be available from your vet.

Worms: Dogs can also carry internal parasites in the form of worms. Ascarid roundworms are the most common. Tapeworms, although less frequent, can be even more debilitating. Heartworms are transmitted by mosquitoes and

Other Vaccines and Treatment

Depending on where you live and your dog's needs, the following ailments and diseases can be treated by your veterinarian.

CONDITION	TREATMENT	PROGNOSIS	RECOMMENDATION
BORDETELLA (KENNEL COUGH)	Keep warm; humidify room; moderate exercise	Highly contagious; rarely fatal in healthy dogs; easily treated	Optional vaccine; prevalence varies; vaccine may be linked to acute reactions; low efficacy
FLEA AND TICK INFESTATION	Topical and ingestible	Highly contagious	Preventive treatment highly recommended
HEARTWORM	Arsenical compound; rest; restricted exercise	Widely occurring infections; regional preventive programs; successful treatment after early detection	Preventive treatment highly recommended
INTESTINAL WORMS	Dewormer; home medication regimen	Good with prompt treatment	Preventive treatment highly recommended
LYME DISEASE (BORRELIOSIS)	Antibiotics	Can't completely eliminate the organism, but can be controlled in most cases	Vaccine recommended only for dogs with high risk of exposure to deer ticks
PARAINFLUENZA	Rest; humidify room; moderate exercise	Highly contagious; mild; self-limiting; rarely fatal	Optional but recommended; doesn't block infection, but lessens clinical signs
PERIODONTITIS	Dental cleaning; extractions; repair	Excellent, but involves anesthesia	Preventive treatment recommended

pose a serious health risk for dogs. Discuss preventives with your veterinarian; some monthly treatments work to protect against heartworm, as well as some of the other common internal parasites.

Depending on where you live, your vet will advise you on the best way to protect your dog from various pests. Because the Shih Tzu is primarily an inside dog and his exposure to wooded areas is fairly limited, you won't have as much cause for concern about ticks and mosquitoes as owners of dogs that spend a great deal of time outdoors. For dogs of all sizes, routine worming is essential throughout their lives. Discuss all parasite-management options with your veterinarian before starting treatment.

Support Canine Health Research

The American Kennel Club Canine Health Foundation (www.akcchf.org) raises money to support canine health research. The foundation makes grants to fund:

- **Identifying the cause(s) of disease**
- **Earlier, more accurate diagnosis**
- **Developing screening tests for breeders**
- **Accurate, positive prognosis**
- **Effective, efficient treatment**

The AKC Canine Health Foundation (AKC CHF) also supports educational programs that bring scientists together to discuss their work and develop new collaborations to further advance canine health.

The AKC created the AKC Canine Health Foundation in 1995 to raise funds to support canine health research. Each year, the AKC CHF allocates $1.5 million to new canine health research projects.

How You Can Help: If you have an AKC-registered dog, submit his DNA sample (cheek swab or blood sample) to the Canine Health Information Center (CHIC) DNA databank (www.caninehealthinfo.org). Encourage regular health testing by breeders, get involved with your local dog club, and support the efforts to host health education programs. And, if possible, make a donation.

For information, contact the AKC Canine Health Foundation, P.O. Box 900061, Raleigh, NC 27675-9061 or check out the website at www.akcchf.org.

SPAY/NEUTER

Fixing your dog plays an important role in responsible dog ownership. Spaying a female dog or neutering a male has more benefits than simply avoiding unwanted puppies. An altered dog will behave better, will be easier to train, and will be less susceptible to some diseases.

If you don't plan to show your Shih Tzu, it's best to have him fixed at the appropriate age that your breeder or veterinarian recommends. Puppies are usually spayed or neutered around five or six months of age; however, if your Shih Tzu is very small, you may be advised to wait until the pup is larger and stronger.

Sometimes health reasons necessitate neutering/spaying—particularly pyometra in females, which will usually require the female's ovaries to be removed. In the case of a male with only one or neither testicle descended into the scrotum, your vet may advise castration to prevent the likelihood of cancer. A benefit of the procedure is the elimination or decreased risk of reproductive cancers and certain other health problems.

FIRST AID

Keeping your Shih Tzu healthy is a matter of keen observation and quick action when necessary. Knowing your dog's normal behaviors will help you to recognize signs of trouble before they become full-blown emergency situations.

Even if the problem is minor, such as a cut or scrape, immediate care will help prevent infection, as well as ensure that your Shih Tzu doesn't make the problem worse by chewing or scratching at it. When caring for a wound, remove

Routine preventive health care will ensure your Shih Tzu will be around for years to come.

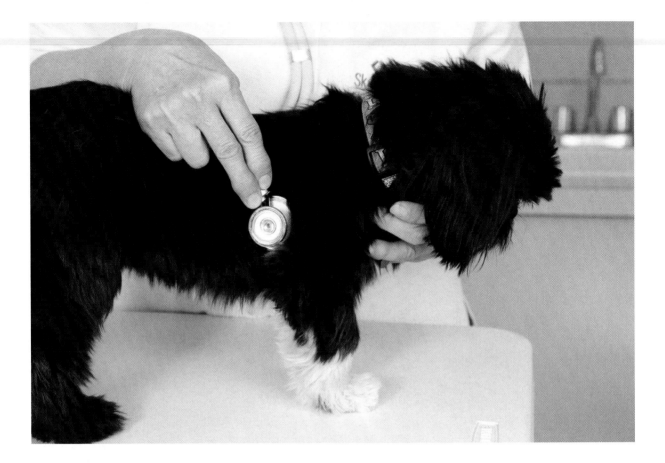

Just like humans, dogs need regular checkups with their doctor. After puppyhood, which requires frequent visits to the vet for booster vaccinations and exams, you should schedule annual checkups for your Shih Tzu.

any splinters or debris, clean with saline solution or warm water, and apply an antibiotic ointment. Bandage the wound if it is on the paw, which can pick up dirt while your dog walks around. It the cut is deep, it may require stitches and should only be treated by a veterinarian.

Consider putting together a basic emergency first-aid kit to keep at home for your dog. Important items to gather include:

- assorted sterile bandages and dressings (including rolls of gauze, which can also be used for a makeshift muzzle)
- an antihistamine (to counteract possible allergic reactions)
- blankets and towels
- disinfectant solution (for flushing out wounds)
- electrolyte solution (for severe dehydration)
- first-aid tape
- ice packs
- name and number of the nearest pet emergency clinic
- a penlight or tiny flashlight
- rolls of sterile cotton
- rubbing alcohol
- scissors (both large and small, blunt-tipped bandage scissors)
- splinting materials
- sterile eye wash or artificial tears
- stethoscope
- thermometer
- tweezers

IN AN EMERGENCY

While anything other than general maintenance should be left to veterinarians, every dog owner should know what to do in case of a canine emergency. Many animal shelters and humane societies offer first-aid classes that teach dog owners to learn how to recognize the symptoms of an emergency, how to treat minor injuries, and much more.

Knowing your Shih Tzu's body and habits is key to his continued health. The earlier you realize that something is wrong with your dog, the better chance your vet has of helping him. By checking over your Shih Tzu's body each week and watching for changes in his behavior, you will be able to let your vet know when there is something wrong with your dog. Keep your vet's emergency phone number on your refrigerator or in your cell phone so that he or she can be contacted right away if an emergency occurs.

CHECKUPS

Most veterinarians recommend at least yearly routine checkups as your Shih Tzu grows up. Your vet will administer any necessary booster vaccinations and give your dog a thorough physical exam, including checking your dog's eyes, ears, and heart. A dental evaluation and possible tooth scraping may also be part of the services. The veterinarian may also recommend blood tests or other additional health checks, if he decides they are necessary. Once your dog is past middle age, your veterinarian may recommend increasing these visits to twice yearly for preventive maintenance.

At a Glance ...

Home care largely affects a dog's health, longevity, and overall quality of life.

. . . .

Discuss the course of vaccinations with your vet so that you know which shots your pup will be getting.

. . . .

Keeping your dog's teeth clean is important. This is especially true with Toy breeds like the Shih Tzu, which are prone to have tooth problems.

. . . .

Both internal and external parasites can have serious consequences, but there are easy and effective ways to prevent the common parasites.

. . . .

Discuss spaying/neutering with your vet. Remember that the procedures offer health benefits, eliminating the risk of certain serious health problems.

. . . .

Know the signs of emergency and basic first-aid techniques for dogs; also have a stocked first-aid kit and your vet's number close by.

. . . .

A healthy adult dog will require a yearly vet visit for a full checkup, including a dental examination. A senior dog may need to visit more frequently as a good preventive measure.

CHAPTER ELEVEN

Keeping Your Shih Tzu Active

While any self-respecting Toy dog's main purpose in life is to be a fabulous and elegant pillow-posing companion (a role they play perfectly), exercise is as important for a tiny dog as it is for a large breed. Although Shih Tzu are small dogs, they are full of verve and energy, and they are perfectly willing and able to lead an active lifestyle. In fact, it's necessary for their overall health and well-being.

Playing with family members is a great way for the Shih Tzu to get some healthy exercise. Make sure to supervise all interactions between small children and dogs.

As a Toy breed with a short muzzle, the Shih Tzu is limited in the duration and extent of exercise he should undertake, so don't expect to take your dog hiking or on a long run along the beach. After all, these little dogs' bodies can only take so much activity before tiring out! But that doesn't mean you can't ever take your Shih Tzu out and about with you for a little fun outdoors. And there are still plenty of organized American Kennel Club sports for him to participate in.

SOMEONE THEIR OWN SIZE

One of the best forms of exercise the Shih Tzu can get is just some good old-fashioned playtime. If you bring two or more Shih Tzu together, they will undoubtedly amuse themselves (and you) for hours, and they will get a chance to exercise their muscles running, jumping, and cavorting. Just be sure your dog doesn't overexert himself while playing with and chasing his playmates. Shih Tzu don't know that they are small dogs, especially when they are puppies, so keep a sharp eye on your feisty puppy any time he plays with larger-breed dogs.

WALK THIS WAY

Dogs kept indoors all day long don't often get all the exercise they need to stay fit and healthy. Luckily, you can help provide that for your pet. The Shih Tzu appreciates going on walks with his owner just as much as the next dog. Taking daily walks is a great way to give your dog the opportunity to investigate new places and new smells and to keep his mind active and his senses alert, all while spending time bonding with you.

Once trained, most Shih Tzu are fairly reliable off lead. But you should make certain that the area where you walk your dog is safe and canine friendly and that you're not disobeying any local leash laws. It is much easier for Shih Tzu groomed in a shorter cut to move around and be active, but those in the long coat can still exercise happily and freely. Just be sure to remove all debris from your dog's coat and give him a thorough brushing after he roams around, to help avoid forming knots and tangles. Because the Shih Tzu's full-length coat touches the ground, it is also important that you don't leave it wet after your dog runs around on damp ground. If you want to keep the coat full length, you may want to learn how to wrap it up to avoid damaging it during free play and exercise. Breeders who show their Shih Tzu in AKC conformation events will know this technique.

If your Shih Tzu is your only pet, you should ideally take him on at least one walk every day. However, if he has other canine company in the home and a large yard where he can exercise, he may not mind going on less frequent outings. Most Shih Tzu adore going on walks with their owners, especially if taken individually. If you have more than one dog in the home, however, traveling in pairs or even larger groups can be a challenge but is possible with well-trained dogs.

THERAPY PETS

Because the Shih Tzu is such an amiable little breed, he tends to get along well with most people, particularly those who love dogs! Quite a few are now used in therapy work, visiting nursing homes and hospitals to provide the residents and patients with a friendly cuddle. The Shih Tzu's charming temperament, coupled with his convenient size and beautiful coat, makes the visit something that many hospital patients and elderly home residents truly enjoy.

If this sounds like something you and your dog want to do, contact the following organizations for more information on how to get started:

• **AKC's Canine Good Citizen® program:** This two-part program requires dogs to pass a ten-step test to receive a certificate rewarding the dog's good manners and preparedness for social interaction within the community. Visit www.akc.org/events/cgc for more information.

• **AKC Therapy Dog program:** This new program recognizes all AKC dog and owner teams that have volunteered their time to help people in therapy work. An official AKC Therapy Dog title (AKC ThD) is awarded to dogs who have been certified by recognized therapy dog associations and have worked to improve the lives of the people they have visited. For more information, go to www.akc.org/akctherapydog.

• **Pet Partners®:** This international nonprofit organization matches people with mental and physical disabilities and patients in health care facilities together with professionally trained animals to help improve the patients' health. Contact them at www.petpartners.org.

• **Therapy Dogs, Inc.:** This organization provides members with registration, support, and insurance while they're involved in animal-assisted volunteer activities. For more information, go to www.therapydogs.com.

Did You Know?

Competitive obedience trials were developed in the 1930s, and the Shih Tzu began competing in the early years. A number of early breeders won advance titles with their dogs, proving from the beginning that the Shih Tzu is more than a pretty chrysanthemum face!

• **Therapy Dogs International:** This nonprofit group helps qualified handlers and their dogs visit facilities and institutions where therapy dogs are needed. Learn how you can get involved by visiting www.tdi-dog.org.

DOG SHOWS

Beyond the everyday exercise options of walking and playing, your Shih Tzu might also enjoy spending time with other people and dogs, while soaking up the limelight competing in dog shows. Conformation is one of the oldest of the AKC's canine competitions, and Shih Tzu shine in the show ring. At a dog show, your Shih Tzu will be examined by a judge to determine how well he conforms to the breed standard (a written description of how the perfect Shih Tzu should look and act). If your dog is registered with the AKC and you want to try your hand at showing, there are organized community events called match or canine experience shows developed specifically for novice exhibitors and their dogs.

If you already know you want to show your Shih Tzu, be sure to look for a show-quality puppy from the start and make your interest known to the breeder. Your Shih Tzu will need to be unaltered (not spayed or neutered), as fixed dogs are not permitted in conformation shows, though they can compete in other AKC sports. Many local clubs host conformation training classes and can help beginners get started with their puppies in this sport.

The AKC's website has extensive information about conformation. First go to www.akc.org/events/conformation/beginners.cfm for information for newcomers. Then, find a nearby match or canine experience show to make your Shih Tzu's debut. Visit www.akc.org/public_education/education_match for help.

JOIN A SPORT

Despite his Toy dog status, the Shih Tzu still competes in many other AKC sports, including both agility and obedience trials. Many owners and trainers have proven

The AKC Code of Sportsmanship

- Sportsmen respect the history, traditions, and integrity of the sport of pure bred dogs.
- Sportsmen commit themselves to values of fair play, honesty, courtesy, and vigorous competition, as well as winning and losing with grace.
- Sportsmen refuse to compromise their commitment and obligation to the sport of purebred dogs by injecting personal advantage or consideration into their decisions or behavior.
- The sportsman judge judges only on the merits of the dogs and considers no other factors.
- The sportsman judge or exhibitor accepts constructive criticism.
- The sportsman exhibitor declines to enter or exhibit under a judge where it might reasonably appear that the judge's placements could be based on something other than the merits of the dogs.
- The sportsman exhibitor refuses to compromise the impartiality of a judge.
- The sportsman respects the American Kennel Club's bylaws, rules, regulations and policies governing the sport of purebred dogs.
- Sportsmen find that vigorous competition and civility are not inconsistent and are able to appreciate the merit of their competition and the efforts of competitors.
- Sportsmen welcome, encourage, and support newcomers to the sport.
- Sportsmen will deal fairly with all those who trade with them.
- Sportsmen are willing to share honest and open appraisals of both the strengths and weaknesses of their breeding stock.
- Sportsmen spurn any opportunity to take personal advantage of positions offered or bestowed upon them.
- Sportsmen always consider as paramount the welfare of their dogs.
- Sportsmen refuse to embarrass the sport, the American Kennel Club, or themselves while taking part in the sport.

that the Shih Tzu can be competitive in these sports. Agility and obedience trials can be enjoyable and challenging for both you and your dog. Some Shih Tzu do quite well in these trials and have made their owners (and the breed) proud.

Obedience: In obedience training, a pup learns to follow basic cues (sit, down, stay, come, etc.), and you learn how to properly give those cues. The benefits of obedience classes are endless. Your dog will be more active, better behaved, and become a model canine citizen. If your Shih Tzu excels in his obedience training classes, consider entering him in an obedience practice match or in the beginner novice class at an obedience trial, which tests dogs to see how well they behave. Obedience trials showcase dogs that have been trained and conditioned to behave well in the home, in public places, and in the presence of other dogs. The sport offers different levels of competition and is great for owners and dogs that prefer to compete against themselves. Learn all about the AKC's obedience program, the sport's history, and the obedience titles that you and your dog can earn at www.akc.org/events/obedience.

Agility: If your little Shih Tzu loves to run and jump, then agility may be a great sport for him. This timed obstacle-course sport for dogs requires your dog to follow a handler's cues as he runs through jumps, tunnels, weave poles, and other objects his little body can maneuver around. Before you simply show up for an event, your Shih Tzu must first learn how to negotiate the obstacles and follow

Always check your Shih Tzu's toys for loose parts or broken, jagged edges that could harm your dog.

Don't let his small size fool you. Shih Tzu love the outdoors and exploring new places. Just don't over exert your tiny Toy dog.

your cues correctly. To do this, you will need to enroll your dog in an agility class. Puppies aren't allowed to begin training until they are at least a year old, but you can begin socializing your dog to the equipment by letting him sniff around a course and by placing him on objects and petting him while he is in place. To find out more about AKC's agility events, go to www.akc.org/events/agility.

Dogs that are comfortable in the show ring still enjoy going on walks and spending one-on-one time with their favorite human.

A WORD OF CAUTION

Regardless of what activities you involve your Shih Tzu in, you can enjoy endless hours of fun together indoors and out. When not sleeping or relaxing, which the

Junior Scholarships

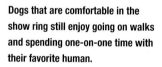

The American Kennel Club shows its commitment to supporting young people in their interest in purebred dogs by awarding thousands of dollars of scholarships to those competing in Junior Showmanship. The scholarships range from $1,000 to $5,000 and are based on a person's academic achievements and his or her history with purebred dogs. Learn more at www.akc.org/kids_juniors.

Shih Tzu does most elegantly, your dog will also enjoy playing with toys around the house. Always remember to check his toys regularly to ensure there are no loose parts that could cause accidental damage or injury.

Shih Tzu should never be allowed to jump down from heights. They may injure their legs or back. Even though your Shih Tzu may think he is perfectly capable, accidents can happen, so keep an eye on him and restrict his access to high places when you're not around to watch over him.

BE YOUR DOG'S BEST FRIEND

Always remember that your Shih Tzu will be happiest when he is spending time with people, especially you. Allow him to join in family activities, while still giving him the freedom to spend time on his own when he wants. Over the centuries, the Shih Tzu has been bred specifically to be an ideal companion. With patience, training, love, and general care, you can ensure your Shih Tzu is around to enjoy your company for years to come.

They may be a "lap-dog" breed, but Shih Tzu love playing outdoors just as much as the next dog. Make sure to provide him with plenty of exercise to stay happy for a lifetime.

At a Glance ...

The small Shih Tzu does not require too much exercise, but activity is good for both physical and mental condition.

. . . .

Off-leash exercise should only be allowed in secure areas. Whether your dog is on or off lead, always be cautious when larger dogs interact with your Shih Tzu.

. . . .

Take precautions for your Shih Tzu's coat when outdoors, and be sure to dry or spot-clean if he gets damp or dirty outdoors.

. . . .

Toy breeds can participate in obedience and agility just as larger dogs can, and the Shih Tzu has potential for success in these sports.

. . . .

Be cautious with toys that you offer to your Shih Tzu because of his uniquely formed bite and small teeth.

Resources

BOOKS

The American Kennel Club's Meet the Breeds: Dog Breeds from A to Z, 4th edition (Irvine, California: I-5 Press, 2014) The ideal puppy buyer's guide, this book has all you need to know about each breed currently recognized by the AKC.

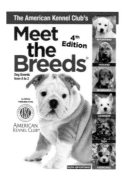

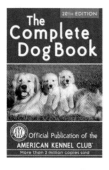

The Complete Dog Book, 20th edition (New York: Ballantine Books, 2006) This official publication of the AKC, first published in 1929, includes the complete histories and breed standards of 153 recognized breeds, as well as information on general care and the dog sport.

The Complete Dog Book for Kids (New York: Howell Book House, 1996) Specifically geared toward young people, this official publication of the AKC presents 149 breeds and varieties, as well as introductory owners' information.

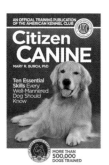

Citizen Canine: Ten Essential Skills Every Well-Mannered Dog Should Know by Mary R. Burch, PhD (Freehold, New Jersey: Kennel Club Books, 2010) This official AKC publication is the definitive guide to the AKC's Canine Good Citizen® Program, recognized as the gold standard of behavior for dogs, with more than half a million dogs trained.

DOGS: The First 125 Years of the American Kennel Club (Freehold, New Jersey: Kennel Club Books, 2009) This official AKC publication presents an authoritative, complete history of the AKC, including detailed information not found in any other volume.

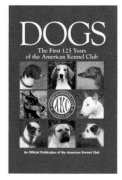

Dog Heroes of September 11th: A Tribute to America's Search and Rescue Dogs, 10th anniversary edition, by Nona Kilgore Bauer (Freehold, New Jersey: Kennel Club Books, 2011) A publication to salute the canines that served in the recovery missions following the September 11th attacks, this book serves as a lasting tribute to these noble American heroes.

The Original Dog Bible: The Definitive Source for All Things Dog, 2nd edition, by Kristin Mehus-Roe (Irvine, California: I-5 Press, 2009) This 831-page magnum opus

includes more than 250 breed profiles, hundreds of color photographs, and a wealth of information on every dog topic imaginable—thousands of practical tips on grooming, training, care, and much more.

PERIODICALS

American Kennel Club Gazette

Every month since 1889, serious dog fanciers have looked to the *AKC Gazette* for authoritative advice on training, showing, breeding, and canine health. Each issue

includes the breed columns section, written by experts from the respective breed clubs. Only available electronically.

AKC Family Dog

This is a bimonthly magazine for the dog lover whose special dog is "just a pet." Helpful tips, how-tos, and features are written in an entertaining and reader-friendly format. It's a lifestyle magazine for today's busy families who want to enjoy a rewarding, mutually happy relationship with their canine companions.

Dog Fancy

The world's most widely read dog magazine, *Dog Fancy* celebrates dogs and the people who love them. Each monthly issue includes info on cutting-edge medical developments, health and fitness (with a focus on prevention, treatment, and natural

therapy), behavior and training, travel and activities, breed profiles and dog news, issues and trends for purebred and mixed-breed dog owners. The magazine informs, inspires, and entertains while promoting responsible dog ownership. Throughout its more than forty-year history, *Dog Fancy* has garnered numerous honors, including being named the Best All-Breed Magazine by the Dog Writers Association of America.

Dogs in Review

For more than fifteen years, *Dogs in Review* has showcased the finest dogs in the United States and from around the world. The emphasis has always been on strong content, with input

from distinguished breeders, judges, and handlers worldwide. This global perspective distinguishes this monthly publication from its competitors—no other North American dog-show magazine gathers together so many international experts to enlighten and entertain its readership.

Dog World Annual

Dog World (formerly *Dogs USA*) is an annual lifestyle magazine published by the editors of *Dog Fancy* that covers all aspects of the dog world: culture, art, history, travel, sports, and science. It also profiles breeds to help prospective owners choose the best dogs for their future needs, such as a potential show champion, super service dog, great pet, or competitive star.

Natural Dog

Natural Dog is the magazine dedicated to giving a dog a natural lifestyle. From nutritional choices to grooming to dog-supply options, this publication helps readers make the transition from traditional to natural methods. The

magazine also explores the array of complementary treatments available for today's dogs: acupuncture,

massage, homeopathy, aromatherapy, and much more. *Natural Dog* is issued as an annual publication and occasionally appears as a special insert section in *Dog Fancy* magazine.

Puppies USA

Also from the editors of *Dog Fancy,* this annual magazine offers essential information for all new puppy owners. *Puppies USA* is lively and informative, including advice on general care, nutrition, grooming, and training techniques for all puppies, whether purebred or mixed breed, adopted, rescued, or purchased. In addition, it offers family fun through quizzes, contests, and much more. An extensive breeder directory is included.

WEBSITES

www.akc.org

The American Kennel Club (AKC) website is an excellent starting point for researching dog breeds and learning about puppy care. The site lists hundreds of breeders, along with basic information about breed selection and basic care. The site also has links to the national breed club of every AKC-recognized breed; breed-club sites offer plenty of detailed breed information, as well as lists of member breeders. In addition, you can find the AKC National Breed Club Rescue List at www.akc.org/breeds/rescue.cfm. If looking for purebred puppies, go to www.puppybuyerinfo.com for AKC classifieds and parent-club referrals.

www.dogchannel.com

Powered by *Dog Fancy,* Dog Channel is "the website for dog lovers," where hundreds of thousands of visitors each month find extensive information on breeds, training, health and nutrition, puppies, care, activities, and more. Interactive features include forums, Dog College, games, and Club Dog, a free club where dog lovers can create blogs for their pets and earn points to buy products. Dog Channel is the one-stop site for all things dog.

www.meetthebreeds.com

The official website of the AKC Meet the Breeds® event, hosted by the American Kennel Club in the Jacob Javits Center in New York City in the fall. The first Meet the Breeds event took place in 2009. The website includes information on every recognized breed of dog and cat, alphabetically listed, as well as the breeders, demonstration facilitators, sponsors, and vendors participating in the annual event.

AKC AFFILIATES

The **AKC Museum of the Dog**, established in 1981, is located in St. Louis, Missouri, and houses the world's finest collection of art devoted to the dog. Visit www.museumofthedog.org.

The **AKC Humane Fund** promotes the joy and value of responsible and productive pet ownership through education, outreach, and grant-making. Monies raised may fund grants to organizations that teach responsible pet ownership; provide for the health and well-being of all dogs; and preserve and celebrate the human-animal bond and the evolutionary relationship between dogs and humankind. Go to www.akchumanefund.org.

The **American Kennel Club Companion Animal Recovery (CAR) Corporation** is dedicated to reuniting lost microchipped and tattooed pets with their owners. AKC CAR maintains a permanent-identification database and provides lifetime recovery services 24 hours a day, 365 days a year, for all animal species. Millions of pets are enrolled in the program, which was established in 1995. Visit www.akccar.org.

The **American Kennel Club Canine Health Foundation (AKC CHF), Inc.** is the largest foundation in the world to fund canine-only health studies for purebred and mixed-breed dogs. More than $22 million has been allocated in research funds to more than 500 health studies conducted to help dogs live longer, healthier lives. Go to www.akcchf.org.

AKC PROGRAMS

The **Canine Good Citizen Program (CGC)** was established in 1989 and is designed to recognize dogs that have good manners at home and in the community. This rapidly growing, nationally recognized program stresses responsible dog ownership for owners and basic training and good manners for dogs. All dogs that pass the ten-step Canine Good Citizen test receive a certificate from the American Kennel Club. Go to www.akc.org/events/cgc.

The **AKC S.T.A.R. Puppy Program** is designed to get dog owners and their puppies off to a good start and is aimed at loving dog owners who have taken the time to attend basic obedience classes with their puppies. After completing a six-week training course, the puppy must pass the AKC S.T.A.R. Puppy test, which evaluates Socialization, Training, Activity, and Responsibility. Go to www.akc.org/starpuppy.

The **AKC Therapy Dog** program recognizes all American Kennel Club dogs and their owners who have given their time and helped people by volunteering as a therapy dog-and-owner team. The AKC Therapy Dog program is an official American Kennel Club title awarded to dogs that have worked to improve the lives of the people they have visited. The AKC Therapy Dog title (AKC ThD) can be earned by dogs that have been certified by recognized therapy dog organizations. For more information, visit www.akc.org/akctherapydog.

Index

AMERICAN KENNEL CLUB®

Advocating for the purebred dog as a family companion, advancing canine health and well-being, working to protect the rights of all dog owners and promoting responsible dog ownership, the **American Kennel Club:**

Sponsors more than **22,000 sanctioned events** annually including conformation, agility, obedience, rally, tracking, lure coursing, earthdog, herding, field trial, hunt test, and coonhound events

Features a **10-step Canine Good Citizen® program** that rewards dogs who have good manners at home and in the community

Has reunited more than **400,000** lost pets with their owners through the AKC Companion Animal Recovery - visit **www.akccar.org**

Created and supports the AKC Canine Health Foundation, which funds research projects using the more than **$22 million** the AKC has donated since 1995 - visit **www.akcchf.org**

Joins **animal lovers** through education, outreach and grant-making via the AKC Humane Fund - visit **www.akchumanefund.org**

We're more than champion dogs. We're the dog's champion.

www.akc.org